THE CULTURAL AND ECONOMIC
CONTEXT OF MATERNAL INFANTICIDE

THE CULTURAL AND ECONOMIC CONTEXT OF MATERNAL INFANTICIDE: A CRYING BABY AND THE INABILITY TO ESCAPE

BY

MARTHA SMITHEY
Texas Tech University, USA

United Kingdom – North America – Japan – India – Malaysia – China

Emerald Publishing Limited
Howard House, Wagon Lane, Bingley BD16 1WA, UK

First edition 2019

British Library Cataloguing in Publication Data
A catalogue record for this book is available from the British Library

ISBN: 978-1-78754-208-2 (Print)
ISBN: 978-1-78743-327-4 (Online)
ISBN: 978-1-78743-951-1 (Epub)

ISOQAR certified
Management System,
awarded to Emerald
for adherence to
Environmental
standard
ISO 14001:2004.

Certificate Number 1985
ISO 14001

INVESTOR IN PEOPLE

This book is dedicated to the babies whose heart-breaking stories help us understand the serious consequences of cultural and economic inequality of women.
For Mom, Marilyn, Hershel, and Luis – the significant forces that shape my life.

Contents

List of Figures

List of Tables

Acknowledgments

This book has been a long-time coming. In many ways, I have shaped and reshaped my seminal work on infanticide in my dissertation at Texas A&M University as I expanded my research into new areas of understanding mothering, the consequences of inequality, and violence. I am deeply grateful to Howard B. Kaplan for successfully guiding me through the application and subsequent expectations of a pre-doctoral fellowship from The National Institute on Drug Abuse (NIDA Award#5F3-DA05463). His teaching and mentoring challenged and inspired me. I am also very grateful to Ben Crouch, Jane Sell, and Alex McIntosh for their support and insights as they shepherded me through my dissertation at Texas A&M University.

From there, I want to thank my colleagues at the University of Texas at El Paso for their support as I continued my work on infanticide and mothering. A special thanks to Howard Daudistel, Kathy Staudt, Roy Malpass, and Andrew Giacomazzi for their friendship and encouragement. I want to also thank Bernard Auchter at the National Institute of Justice who always supported and encouraged my research for this and other projects.

A sincere thank you to Susanne E. Green for a lifelong friendship and to whom I know I can turn to whenever I feel overwhelmed.

My colleagues at Texas Tech University gave me the support and academic space to organize years of work into this book. I want to give a special thanks to Tamra Walter for the years of friendship, support, and much-needed laughter about academia and life in general.

Finally, I wish to thank my family for their love and patience as I made extra demands on them while struggling with the research and writing. Their love and support is the motivation for all I do in my life. Raising my son, Hershel, has taught me more about the reality of mothering than anything I have studied or heard. He is an amazing person and, despite my frequent fumbling through motherhood, has become the most humane and caring person I know. He is the work about which I am most proud. My husband and colleague, Ignacio Luis Ramirez, is the perfect life partner for me. His love, sense of adventure, and insights into my life at home and work are invaluable.

Chapter 1

An Introduction and Overview of Infanticide

Infanticide has a lengthy history reaching back to ancient societies (Knight, 1991). In many instances, it was the result of socially sanctioned religious sacrifice, economy to ensure the survival of existing family members, or disposal of physically defective infants (deMause, 1988; Dorne, 1989; Newman, 1978; Radbill, 1987). This practice was common in ancient Greece, Rome, and early German society. During the Middle Ages, infanticide was occurring in every country in Europe (deMause, 1988). Often the practice of female infanticide was condoned as a form of population control. For example, China is a nation well known for the commission of infanticide by their citizenry. In China, it has been estimated that tens of thousands of female infants were murdered due to the cultural beliefs that sons bestow blessings on the family and that females are economic liabilities due to dowries and their departure from the home and extended family care when they marry. But more notorious, and a possibly bigger cause of female infanticide, has been the government's one-child policy instituted in 1979 but officially revoked in 2013 (Zhu, 2003). This policy was designed to curtail the untenable population growth of the past few decades. The intent of the policy is to reduce births by rewarding families for limiting family size to one child. It interacted with the cultural beliefs regarding the rewards of a son and the costs of a daughter to create a serious infanticide trend of eliminate female babies. The effects of the policy lasted through 2015 as the Chinese government had to reeducate citizens toward different cultural beliefs to stop female infanticide.

This history attributes causes of infanticide to the social forces of government policy, economic, need and cultural expectations. In this book, I explain how two of these social forces – economic need and cultural expectations – persist in modern-day maternal infanticide. I begin by introducing and defining infanticide, discussing the debate whether maternal love and "instinct" are natural or social forces, and describing the nature and trends of the occurrence of infanticide. I conclude with a brief discussion of mental illness as a cause of infanticide, which is beyond the scope of this book.

In this chapter, I introduce and define infanticide, discuss the debate whether maternal love and "instinct" are natural or social forces, describe the nature and trends of its occurrence, and conclude with a discussion of mental illness, which is beyond the scope of this book. The medical community defines "infant" as 12 months and countries with infanticide laws default to the medical community. In the United States, there are no infanticide laws to legally define but use of the term in the legal community generally refers to 12 months. In historical and literary works, an "infant" is a physically, cognitively, and emotionally underdeveloped being. My original work on this phenomenon (Smithey, 1994) developed a sociological perspective on mother-perpetrated infanticide in which I argue that post-partum psychosis and other forms of mental illness do not sufficiently explain most cases of infanticide and that cultural expectations and social inequalities are more powerful explanations. Within this analytical frame, I used the more literary inclusive definition of infanticide by broadening the possibility of infanticide of children from ages 1 day to 36 months. This age range was determined by the potential for post-partum hormone fluctuations lasting up to 36 months (with most causes resolving within 24 months). That research, subsequent research by myself, and published works by others inform this book (Adinkrah, 2001; Alder & Baker, 1997; Arnot, 1994; Briggs & Mantini-Briggs, 2000; d'Orban, 1979; Friedman, Horwitz, & Resnick, 2005; Jackson, 2002; Mugavin, 2005; Oberman, 2003; Oberman & Meyer, 2001, 2008; Rodriguez & Smithey, 1999; Rose, 1986; Scott, 1973; Smithey, 1994, 1998; Smithey & Ramirez, 2004; Stroud, 2008; and others).

The scope of this book is the commission of lethal assault of a child under three years of age by the biological mother. It does not cover the death of an infant less than 24 hours (i.e., neonaticide) because my theory assumes the mother intended to keep and raise the child. I exclude officially diagnosed clinical cases of mental illness that clearly precede the conception of the infant. I omit these cases in an attempt to focus solely on social factors. I exclude clinical cases of post-partum depression and psychosis. These disorders are caused by hormonal imbalances as the mother's body attempts to readjust to prepregnancy hormone levels (Daniel & Lessow, 1964). I do not include murder-suicide, although social forces causing suicide have been studied at least since Durkheim (1879), maybe before, it is difficult in fatalistic suicide cases to separate fully clinical mental forces from social causes for each and every case. The use of second-hand data is problematic for establishing valid, temporal order. The research on this type of infanticide (e.g., Alder & Baker, 1997) points to overwhelmingly hopelessness and depression as the cause of the murder. The interactions of these causes are valid and require a different, complex theory and analysis than I have done. Finally, I do not attempt to explain infanticide by other perpetrators in this book. I have begun collecting studies, court manuscripts, and qualitative interview data with biological fathers, stepfathers, and mother's boyfriends who have committed infanticide. That work is in progress.

1.1. Maternal Love: Instinctual or Cultural?

The relative ease with which mothers have been able to murder their children in the past is a function of their ability to emotionally distance themselves from the child. Immediately upon birth, most infants were drowned or left to die from exposure seemingly without serious trauma to the parents. Sociohistorical researchers often view this as a lack of maternal love. For example, Shorter (1975) argues that mothers did not have "maternal love" for their infants. He argues that it developed in the last quarter of the eighteenth century and, in some social classes, even later. He attributes its development and high-priority emotional status of mothers to modernization.

> Good mothering is an *invention* of modernization. In traditional society, mothers viewed the development and happiness of infants younger than two with indifference. In modern society, they place the welfare of their small children above all else. (p. 168)

He further states that traditional mothers did not see their infants as human beings. Parents were not able to emotionally empathize with the infant. The emergence of maternal love occurred only when mothers reordered their priorities, primarily due to romantic love unseating arranged marriages, and put the welfare of the infant above "material circumstances and community attitudes (that forced them) to subordinate infant welfare to other objectives, such as keeping the farm going or helping their husbands weave cloth" (p. 169).

deMause (1988) asserts the "natural" attachment, that is, maternal instinct, modern mothers have to their babies is not natural instinct but rather is based on a psychohistorical change in perception and the lack of a need for distancing. Wall (2001) similarly argues, "Cultural understandings of maternal instinct and love are connected to the popular and scientific notions of attachment and bonding" (p. 10). Birth control practices have gradually become more effective and acceptable in the religious sphere thus reducing the economic and population strain placed on many families and societies and the possibility of infanticide has for those purposes has lessened. However, modern maternal attachment, empathy, and effective birth control have not totally eradicated infanticide.

The occurrence of infanticide has had a significant, enduring trend that in the past century has declined due to advances in understanding and controlling human reproduction. That infanticide continues to occur has not changed. What has changed, and perhaps is new, are the cultural acceptance, beliefs, and social conditions under which it occurs.

Cultural changes have led to the belief that "child homicide" is "the antithesis of usual responses to childhood, quintessentially the time of nurture and development, of vulnerability and dependence" (Stroud, 2008, p. 482). However, the assumed sanctity of maternal instinct remains unquestioned despite history not necessarily supporting it. In fact, the belief is a prominent force used when judging or questioning how much a mother loves her child. Complete and total bonding with the baby at birth is presumed to be automatic and mothers who do not totally sacrifice all they have from that day forward are judged negatively and possibly labeled "bad mother" overall.

I contend, as do other family researchers (e.g., Badinter, 1978; Hays, 1996; Kitzinger, 1989; Oakley, 1974) and historians (deMause, 1988; Shorter, 1975) that maternal love is not automatic and is a social construct that is not founded in nature. Social forces are just as, or possibly more, powerful over individuals as natural forces. Suicide, whether fatalistic or altruistic (Durkheim, 1897), is a prime example of social forces overpowering the natural force of survival. But regardless of whether maternal love is founded in nature or is socially constructed, the expectation is the same – mothers are expected to fully love their children and place all else above them. Girls are gender socialized into this expectation and it is the foundation of modern mothering ideology. *Infanticide is the most egregious mother norm violation possible in modern society.* The seriousness of the maternal love norm makes understanding infanticide in modern society important for many reasons. Besides the obvious need to prevent the deaths of children, understanding infanticide and the social construction of "good mothering" is essential to understanding women's economic and cultural inequality that is institutionalized by this belief. Men are not held to this level of sacrifice for their children. This difference upholds patriarchy and the subordination of women, especially mothers.

This work on infanticide contributes to our understanding of mother–infant interactions in several ways. One, I connect the unrealistic, disorganized state of the mothering ideology to the direct consequence of a breakdown in mother–infant interactions – the death of the infant. Two, I make salient the impact of the content of "good mothering" expectations on mothers. This largely untested content comprises the mothering ideology and is promoted by the capitalistic enterprise of the child-rearing industry and the media. Three, I connect family violence and intimate partner violence to infanticide – another facet of the cycle of violence. Four, I expose yet another negative consequence of gender economic and cultural inequality. The valid and large amount of research and data on these inequalities experienced by females has not been incorporated into mainstream criminology to explain female-perpetrated infanticide. Extant research on poverty and violence toward children shows that criminology has high potential for understanding this type of crime (Jensen, 2001) but it must embrace also the cultural and social inequalities of mothering. Generally, mainstream criminology fails to address gendered economic hardship despite feminist research showing that women are more likely to experience fewer economic resources and experience higher rates of poverty than men (Bianchi, 2000). The inability to provide for basic needs produces stress and frustration that creates a demoralizing environment potentially resulting in aggression (Messner & Rosenfeld, 1997). Five, I provide a detailed view of the effects of stress on women and offer that these stressors operate as a range from the "normal" stress to "dangerous" stress of childrearing. I suggest that any mother could commit violence toward her baby. Placing normal people in abnormal circumstances can lead to violence, especially mothers experiencing a significant lack of economic resources. Six, I bring to light a dire consequence of socially coercing and forcing women to raise unplanned, unwanted babies. Finally, I provide windows to opportunities for preventing violence against children, including nonlethal violence.

1.2. Trends: How Often Does Maternal Love Go Wrong?

Several studies find that infants under the age of 12 months have a higher risk of homicide than children of other ages (Abel, 1986; McCleary & Chew, 2002; Overpeck, 2003; Rodriguez & Smithey, 1999). In fact, the first 24 hours of life carries a risk of homicide that is comparable to homicide rates of adolescents (FBI Uniform Crime Report, 2015) and is more than twice the national incidence (Crandall, Chiu, & Sheehan, 2006). I collected demographic data on 380 cases of infanticide for the years 1985 through 1990 in Texas (Smithey, 1994, 1998) and find that newborns have the highest risk of lethal injury (see Table 1.1).

Studying official data in the United Kingdom, Brookman and Nolan (2006) find that of the children killed between 1995 and 2002, more than one-third was under the age of 12 months.

Official crime data show that infant homicide has declined in the United States. Figure 1.1 shows a 54% decline the number of infants less than 12 months of age murdered over the past two decades. It must be noted, however, that this is the smallest age interval given in the official crime data. All other age intervals range from 4 to 10 years. Considering proportionality of the interval, Craig's (2004) finding that "the risk of becoming the victim of homicide is much greater for infants than another age group" (p. 57) still holds.

Table 1.1. Distribution of Infanticide Victims' Ages in Texas, 1985–1990.

	f	%	Cum %
Victim's Age in Months			
Newborn	38	10.05	10.05
0.06–3.74	70	18.52	28.57
4–6.75	48	12.70	41.27
7–9.75	37	9.79	51.06
10–12.75	31	8.20	59.26
13–15.75	37	9.79	69.05
16–18.75	31	8.20	77.25
19–21.75	19	5.03	82.28
22–24.75	37	9.79	92.06
25–27.75	8	2.12	94.18
28–30.75	19	5.03	99.21
31–34	3	0.79	100.00
Total	378	100.00	

Notes: Mean = 11.06 months; Median = 9.25 months; Standard deviation = 9.04.

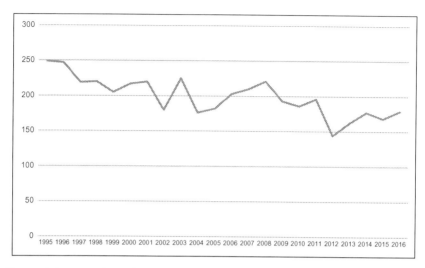

Figure 1.1.   Number of Homicide Victims in the US < One Year of Age. *Source*: FBI *Crime in the United States*, 1995–2016.

Children are more likely to be killed by their parent than by a stranger or other type of offender (Schwartz & Isser, 2007) and mothers are the most likely offenders (Smithey, 1998). Brookman and Nolan (2006) find that when the perpetrator is female, there is a 90% chance it is the mother (p. 873). However, biological fathers and stepfathers combined make up only 83% of male perpetrators. In my research, mothers are the likely offenders until age four months, when fathers became the likely offenders until six months, then a combination of mothers, fathers, stepfathers, and mother's boyfriends became almost equally likely to the offender until age 25 months. At that age and until age 32 months, mothers were the most likely offender (Smithey, 1994, 1998). Overall, the studies find that mothers are the most likely offender of filicides less than three years of age.

The chances of infanticide are higher for babies that are atypically ill or "colicky." Colic occurs in up to 28% of infants across all categories of gender, race, and social class (Gottesman, 2007, p. 334). Studying mothers of colicky infants, Levitzky and Cooper (2001) find that 70% of mothers of colicky infants had explicit aggressive thoughts toward their infants and 26% of these mothers had infanticidal thoughts during the infant's episodes of colic (p. 117).

The studies on whether male or female infants are at greater risk of infanticide have produced mixed results. Some studies find no significant differences in whether the victim is male or female (Chew, McCleary, Lew, & Wang, 1999; Smithey, 1999). Brookman and Nolan (2006) conclude the gender of the victim varies by the gender of the offender with female-perpetrated infanticide not being victim-gendered but male-perpetrated infanticide tends to happen to male infants. Earlier research by Overpeck (2003) reports a slight favoring of male victims by 10% but this includes male and female offenders. Just 10 years prior, Abel (1986) found no distinction of victims by gender.

Chew et al. (1999) find that nearly one-half of the offenders are non-Hispanic, white. I collected demographic data on 380 infanticide cases in the Texas for the years 1985–1990 (Smithey, 1994, 1999). In these data, the largest category of race and ethnicity is white (42.71%) followed by African American (35.28%) and Mexican Origin (21.75%). The percent African American victims is disproportionately high for Texas. The demographic for the state was 11.9 during this time interval (Census of Population, 1990). Percent Mexican American or Mexican Origin (21.75%) is slightly under the percent for the state (25.5%).

Given the isolation of the mother and infant, children are most likely to be killed at home (Chew et al., 1999). This mirrors the findings from nonlethal child abuse (Gelles & Straus, 1988; Straus & Gelles, 1990). Infants tend to be killed with personal weapons, such as hands, feet, or body mass. The most frequent lethal injury is a blow to the head resulting in cerebral hemorrhage (Abel, 1986; Crandall et al., 2006; DiMaio & DiMaio, 2001). Other studies report that personal weapons are the most frequently used in infanticide and child homicide (Abel, 1986; Smithey, 2001). Table 1.2 shows the causes of deaths in 380 homicides of infants less than 34 months of age.

Table 1.2. Cause of Death among Children under 34 Months of Age.

	f	%
Head trauma	206	54.21
Body trauma	38	10.00
Abdomen trauma	30	7.89
Asphyxia	24	6.32
In-utero injury	13	3.42
Exposure/abandonment	12	3.16
Stab/cut	11	2.89
Gunshot wound	11	2.89
Scalding	8	2.11
Arson	7	1.84
Neglect/malnutrition	6	1.58
Motor vehicle impact	6	1.58
Drowning	5	1.32
Drug/medication overdose	2	0.53
In-utero cocaine overdose	1	0.26
Total	380	100.00

Source: Smithey (1994).

More often than not, autopsies show no history of abuse toward the infant. In order for an autopsy to detect episodes of violence prior to the lethal injury, the earlier violence would have to be severe enough to leave bruises or broken bones, signs of neglect, and degrees of chronic dehydration and malnutrition. About one-third of autopsies of homicide victims under age two show bruises and broken bones in various stages of healing (DiMaio & DiMaio, 2001; Knight, 1991; Smithey, 1994). What autopsies do not detect is less severe violence. This can include bruising that happened several weeks before the baby's death and the bruises have healed completely. The healing of broken or fractured bones or ribs will leave permanent, detectable change that can be prior violence depending on the anatomical harmony with the story given by the parents for the injury. The other forms of violence that autopsies may not detect include minor physical assault without bruising, emotional abuse, acute neglect, and lack of medical care. Researching these forms of prior violence requires social service and psychological history reviews in child homicide cases. These too find that most cases have no history of abuse.

The leading cause of infanticide is head trauma (54.21%) (Smithey, 1994, 1998). Head trauma typically occurred in three forms: (1) a blow to the head via an adult fist or foot; (2) slamming the infant against a wall, floor, table, or bathtub; and (3) severe shaking of the infant causing the brain to swell. The distant, second largest category is body/abdomen trauma (10.00%). This type of fatal trauma tends to be the result of a general battering which results in multiple injuries. Other causes of death, such as asphyxia, exposure due to abandonment, stab wounds, gunshot wounds, burns, and neglect, are less than 8%. Asphyxia and exposure due to abandonment tend to be a more passive act of violence, as compared with physical assault, with the offender suffocating the victim by placing his/her hand over the mouth or submerging the victim in water. Gunshot wounds and burns are highly violent, physical injuries. While not a physical battering or acute injury, neglect, malnutrition, and dehydration are active, slow, torturous deaths. They are crimes of omission, but they are not passive in the same manner as suffocation or exposure.

The official crime and research data cited here likely underestimate the amount of infant homicides in the United States. This is particularly true for neonaticides. It is impossible to estimate the number of successfully concealed pregnancies and disposed newborns occurring annually since the data rely on the recording of a birth to know if a baby is missing or locating an abandon infant. Valid estimates are extremely difficult due to this reason. Medical and government data collection organizations and academic researchers have made very little progress toward valid estimates.

Infanticide cases where the baby's birth is known and registered are also underestimated. Two major reasons for this are misdiagnosis of Sudden Infant Death Syndrome (SIDS) and unqualified death certifiers. Emery and Taylor (1986) predict that as many of 10% of SIDS cases could be homicides or at least not due to natural causes, which is the manner of death classification for SIDS. The nonnatural manners of death are suicide, homicide, accident, or undetermined. While it is possible that some infant homicides are accidents, the inability to accurately determine a cause and manner of death speaks to possible, significant inaccuracies in the data.

The prevalent inaccuracy in misdiagnosed manners of death of infants is most likely due to rulings of SIDS. Most estimates of infant homicides diagnosed as SIDS are conservative and they underestimate homicides by at least 5% (Brookman & Nolan, 2006). Also, deaths due to suffocation where there have not been postmortem findings to indicate a cause of death, have been misdiagnosed as SIDS (Stanton & Sampson, 2002).

Work by myself and a colleague addressing qualifications and death certification (Smithey & Ramirez, 2004) finds that levels of suspicion of the events of an infant death less than one year of age varied significantly by the amount of death certification training and education the certifier had, and whether they were a coroner or medical examiner. As expected, medical examiners and coroners with higher levels of death certification training were more suspicious of reported injuries leading to death. We conclude that the likelihood of underestimated infant homicides is high given that approximately one-fourth of the geographical United States has death certification by underqualified, untrained death certifiers. A total of 13% of the certifiers reported no training at all. To illustrate the seriousness of this circumstance, one death certifier reports that he had a high school diploma, worked full-time at a fast-food chain, and part-time as the county coroner.

Our analysis shows that the odds of medical examiners viewing the scenarios of infant deaths as suspicious enough to warrant further investigation are 66–80% higher than the level of suspicion by coroners. Specifically, the odds of not viewing a sudden, unexpected death occurring while the infant was alone in the bed as an accident double with each additional hour of training. This potentially reflects trained certifiers' perception of the death as natural, however, a ruling of SIDS requires a "negative" autopsy where all possible causes of death are ruled out (American Academy of Pediatrics, 2001; DiMaio & DiMaio, 2001). Such a determination requires an extensive investigation for validation of the cause of death. As such, certifiers educated in forensic pathology or trained in death investigation have been taught to not *initially* rule an infant death as SIDS without ruling out all other possible causes. However, coroners with low levels or no training in death certification were found to be unlikely to do this (Smithey & Ramirez, 2004).

1.3. Is It Mental Illness?

Another important issue in understanding maternal infanticide is mental illness. When I first began studying mothers who kill their infants, I found the explanation of mental illness to be unsatisfactory or an insufficient causative factor. After years of study, I now know that the medical, psychological, psychiatric, and even family violence literature did little to address directly the social conditions and forces that construct the inequalities and cause the suffering of mothers. In fact, the family violence literature, while addressing some of the same social conditions found as causative in this book, tends to portray infanticide and child homicide by parents in general as accidental deaths due to abuse (see Gelles, 1991). In other words, there may have been intent to assault and batter the child but not to kill it. While this field of study has moved away from this, there are two lasting effects. One, the casting of the homicides as "accidental" diminishes their significance and suggests that the family violence and child abuse theories are sufficient for understanding their occurrence. We must look to more comprehensive causes to understand the larger context of child abuse and homicide. This leads to the second effect, which is a lack of focus on the mothering ideology and the cultural and economic inequalities it produces as possible causes of violence against children. The history of portraying violent women as "mad" or "bad" is a dichotomy that assumes uniformity in types of perpetrators. Dichotomies fail to capture the reality and complexity of motive, which includes variation in motive, interpersonal skills, self-discipline, interpretation of infant's actions, etc. Infanticide must be examined as a continuum of intersecting personal qualities, life experiences, resources, social constraints, and social expectations. Also, the calls for classification or types of risk factors reduce important differences in understanding motive and preventing infanticide. I discuss this in the last chapter.

Researchers debate mental illness as a causative factor in mother-perpetrated infant deaths (e.g., Alder & Baker, 1997; Oberman, 2003; Oberman & Meyer, 2001; Smithey, 1994; Stanton & Simpson, 2002; Stanton & Skipworth, 2005). It is one of several classifications of infanticide and filicide used by researchers, including those in the fields of psychology, psychiatry, or social work (e.g., Bourget & Gagne, 2005). d'Orban's (1979) six classifications of infanticide and filicide includes battering mothers, neonaticides, retaliating mothers, women who kill unwanted children, mercy killings, and *mothers who are mentally ill.* The distinctiveness of these categories makes clear that mental illness is only one of several causes of infanticide.

It is hard to find clear boundaries by which to group mental health issues in infanticide cases. Mental illness cases call for a significantly different understanding and response than cases of instrumentally eliminating an unwanted child or the "impulse" homicides discussed in this book. From my research and from studying the work of others, I find it useful to categorize mental illness, as it is associated with maternal infanticide, into three groups. First, mental illness diagnosed prior to the birth of the infant and mental illness that is due to hormonal imbalances during the pregnancy and for a few months following the birth, such as post-partum depression or psychosis. I do not include these cases in this book nor do I include findings of mental illness as a causative factor from other studies in my analytical portrayal of the socially situated context of infanticide. I cite social correlates from some studies on mental illness and filicide (killing one's children) but with the intent of including only those correlates that are common to most mothers (including mothers who have not injured or hurt their children). While the findings on mental illness prior to committing infant homicide in the medical and psychiatric literature are mixed (Craig, 2004, p. 59), there are cases of infanticide where mothers were classified as mentally ill prior to pregnancy. Studies indicate a range of prevalence from 10% to 15% of infanticides. This is likely an underestimate given the lack of accessible mental and pre-/postnatal healthcare in our society. But a prevalence range of 85–90% nonclinical cases strongly indicates factors other than mental illness. Craig (2004) finds that women are at 25 times more likely to become psychotic in the month following childbirth and 10–15% of mothers have an episode of major depression in the year after giving birth compared to nonchild-bearing women (p. 59).

Maushart (1999) challenges the validity of most psychiatric diagnoses and claims "traditional psychotherapy sustains itself by mother-blaming" (p. 18). Mental illness has been used to control women for centuries and, in practice, many women have been mislabeled. It has been used to regulate women's sexuality, reduce access to economic wealth and success, to keep women in a lower social status (especially poor and minority women), and to maintain the power of men. As found by Walmsley (2000), mental illness is a key motivating factor in the regulation of mostly poor and working-class women.

There has been insufficient discussion of the social forces beyond the mother's control that may make her mentally unwell or that put her in survival mode with copious amounts of emotion work to avoid becoming or appearing mentally ill. It is no surprise that disciplines tend to be reductionist and that mental health studies use clinical samples and focus on criteria that determine the type of mental illness, disorder, or disease suspected. As research has become more multidisciplinary and collaborative, there is wider acceptance now of the conceptualization of mental illness as a result of the interaction of environmental stress and individual vulnerability and that it arises out of and causes social adversity (e.g., see Stanton & Simpson, 2002, pp. 10–11). Unemployment is now recognized as a stress factor linked to the onset of psychological problems (Stroud, 2008, p. 490).

The largely discipline-driven methods of psychology give, at best, secondary consideration to needed social change of life circumstances beyond an individual's control, such as economic and cultural inequality. These circumstances can cause acute or severe mental illness that can cause people to "lose it" and become violent. This is my second group of mental illness: the "lose it" category of mothers who arguably may have acute mental illness or at least mental distress due to the social stressors and situated context of mothering at the time they assault their infants. In other words, the stress of meeting the social, anomic, unrealistic expectations of mothering to fulfill a core identity that is socialized into girls – *be a good mother* – can make a mother mentally ill or have symptoms of mental illness. The expectations of motherhood can be and often is dangerous to women's mental health (Maushart, 1999). This book addresses these mothers.

The third group is mothers who experience intense, chronic anger and frustration who, on some level, use lethal, instrumental violence to "solve the problem" of unwanted children by eliminating them. In some cases, the instrumental violence is revenge toward the other parent (d'Orban, 1979). These cases suggest a degree of premeditation and agency on the part of the mother. I include these cases and struggle to separate them from the "lose it" impulse homicides. This struggle is due mostly to the data available. Driven by legal definitions, qualitative and quantitative studies tend to use the post hoc definition of homicide or murder. For this definition, the difference between a homicide and an assault is death. In all types of homicides, the event is labeled a homicide only if someone dies and the "homicide victim" is the person who died. Only in a few cases is self-defense recognized and even then the dead person is still referred to as the victim. The precariousness of whether a person injured from assault lives or dies, the most significant of which is the timeliness of medical attention, makes the definition post hoc. Another less significant factor relevant to the definition of homicide is the intensity of the assault does not produce a linear outcome of lethality. A seemingly "light" assault can be just as deadly as a severe, intense beating if the injured party happens to trip or hit their head on a hard surface as opposed to a softer surface. The data from the criminal justice system, social services, medical facilities, protective services, and death certifiers all have this inherent problem. Moreover, these data sources are coded and classified by human beings who very much view the actions of the offender through the lens of the normative expectations of being a good person. The diagnosis of the mother as mentally ill is confounded with the act of murdering her child due to belief in maternal instinct and automatic maternal attachment. People who hold this belief find it very plausible that only a mentally ill or defective mother would kill her child. Additionally, in cases of filicide, diagnoses of mental illness are unreliable and vary from "decade to decade and country to country" (Mugavin, 2005, p. 66). Consequently, there is no valid way to determine if the mental illness existed prior to the pregnancy, birth, or death of the child. For women, this includes the gendered, very significant social role and identity of being a good mother. I discuss this role and identity extensively in Chapter 3.

Most cases of infanticide or child homicide are not due to previously diagnosed mental illness (Crittenden & Craig, 1990; Smithey, 1994; Stroud, 2008). They fall into the second or third group or both. The problem with trying to identify a person and "treating" them as mentally ill is that this adds to the denial of the social forces of contradictory, unclear, unrealistic mothering. Infanticide is a problem that needs to be addressed at the social-structural level with a strong focus on gender inequality, not medicalized. To send mothers message that they may be mentally ill or are becoming mentally ill, is to add stress and confusion to the cultural inequality of mothering. Labeling a desperate, struggling mother mentally ill is not a solution. But it is our preference. People want to believe that anyone deemed responsible for the murder of an infant, especially when the murder is by parents or close caretakers, must be mentally ill.

As previously pointed out, there are cases of infanticide due to mental illness. For women who suffer from mental illness and post-partum depression or psychosis due to hormonal imbalances, the psychiatric and psychological focus is extremely important and care for these women must be provided. The lack of mental health care is yet another social force beyond individual control and is part of the inequality experienced by women and children, especially minorities.

1.4. Central Theme and Organization of This Book

The medical and psychiatric fields dominated the study of infanticide and filicide for several decades and explained its occurrence as the result of post-partum psychosis or mental illness. In the past three decades, a sociological lens has been placed on this crime. However, extant studies on infanticide and filicide that address the social conditions typically take the mother or parents having unrealistic expectations of parenting as a given and not in need of explanation. A large amount of social and behavioral science research offers detailed data, trends, and descriptive analysis on infanticide (Adinkrah, 2001; Alder & Baker, 1997; Arnot, 1994; Briggs & Mantini-Briggs, 2000; Crimmins, Langley, Brownstein, & Spunt, 1997; d'Orban, 1979; Fiala & LaFree, 1988; Freidman et al., 2005; Gartner & McCarthy, 2006; Hewitson, 2000; Jackson, 2002; Kunz & Bahr, 1996; Mouzos, 2000; Mugavin, 2005; Oberman, 2003; Oberman & Meyer, 2001, 2008; Rodriguez & Smithey, 1999; Rose, 1986; Schwartz & Isser, 2007; Scott, 1973; Smithey & Ramirez, 2004; Stanton & Simpson, 2002; Stroud, 2008; and more). However, this sizeable body of research does not adequately detail the intensifying behavioral exchanges between the mother and child that result in a fatal event nor does it sufficiently addressed the source of the unrealistic expectations or the cause of the confused contradictory schemas used by mothers when self-evaluating their own parenting actions or when interpreting the actions of their infant. Extant research tends to assume that violence toward children is due to "poor problem-solving" skills on the part of the parent. These studies accurately portray the interactions that lead to violence, but they fall short in fully explaining how the larger, social contexts in which mothers must operate contribute to her lethal violence. This book addresses this gap in research.

Deconstructing the context of infanticide and stressors related to infanticide will help us redefine intervention efforts, use resources more effectively, and direct us toward needed social change. I address part of the complex problem of the social dimensions of mothering but race, patriarchy, religion, and other social and psychological factors affect each caregiving interaction between a mother and here infant and warrant more attention than given her. Rather, I extensively examine the cultural goals and expectations of what a good mother must achieve in each immediate instance of caregiving: a happy, healthy baby. A crying baby challenges this achievement.

I begin by describing the predispositional and the macro- and micro-social processes of infanticide in Chapter 2. I argue that gender inequality in the economic social institution, especially mommy-tracking, leaves mothers with insufficient resources for raising happy, healthy children. I then describe the predisposing factors of experiencing family violence as a child and intimate partner violence. Next, I present a framework for situating unwanted children and the reality of parenting in the context of infanticide. I close this chapter by focusing on the social isolation and lack of family support in these cases.

In Chapter 3, I explain how the belief in automatic maternal attachment and the subsequent mothering ideology creates a cultural inequality for women that leave them with the difficult and time-consuming task of child rearing. The ideology of mothers is based on middle-class standards that lower classes cannot possibly meet and that middle classes struggle to meet. I argue that while the mothering ideology is a powerful and coercive force for what constitutes a "good mother" and a "happy baby," the child-rearing industry that guards the "stock of knowledge" of mothering has contributed to anomia of the ideology. I explain the mother identity and describe how the institutionalized mothering ideology controls mothers to the point of powerlessness and how social services and the criminal justice system enforce the ideology and, subsequently, keep mothers powerless. I close with how all of this creates a demoralizing context in which mothers attempt to have happy, healthy babies.

In Chapters 4 and 5, I offer a specific framework for understanding the every-day mother–infant interactions that have the potential for lethal violence. I use Luckenbill's situated transaction model of homicide (1977) to explain the stages and escalation of violence in the mother–infant fatal interaction. I present a theoretically integrated model of Mead's (1934) game and role-taking, Goffman's (1959, 1967) saving face and presentation of self, Berger and Luckmann's (1966) social constructionism, and Giddens (1979) structured action and work on power of social institutions over individuals. I explain how the internalization of societal norms of good mothering is part of the social institution of parenting and argue that these norms lead to an emotional intensification of aggressive behavior toward the infant due to an inability meet the expectations. In this case, infant's actions, most commonly crying, are significant symbols that challenge the self-interpretation of the mother's identity as a "good mother." Finally, mothers are culturally and legally not allowed to escape the context of an inconsolable baby and are often socially isolated. In their isolation, they experience asking for help as a humiliating experience but most do it anyway. Unfortunately, in the cases studied here, these calls were not adequately addressed.

In Chapter 6, I offer suggests for prevention and needed social change. I closed by asking the hard questions that we as a society must face if we want to be more humane, equitable, and caring of families and children.

Chapter 2

Predispositional Factors in Maternal Infanticide

My boyfriend didn't help me with money and I couldn't work with two babies. Me and my boyfriend, my baby's daddy, had an argument about friends coming by. Then I fed the babies, bathed them, and put them down for a nap. At noon he (the boyfriend) beat me up, knocked out some of my teeth (she points to gaps in her teeth). I wanted this man out of my life. I would look at the baby and cry and ask why did I have to have this baby? All he did was cry. He wouldn't eat, he wouldn't sleep. I just wanted to go. The baby awaked from his nap and started crying. The baby was on the couch when I hit him. I hit him with the back of my hand on the side. I put him back on the couch and he started crying, then I shook him and starting hitting him. My other baby (two years old) started crying and pulling on my shirt. I started hugging him (the two-year-old). The baby finally cried himself back to sleep and my older baby went into the living room. My boyfriend came back over and took care of the baby and put him to bed. Next morning, the kids got up, the baby wouldn't eat. I left the apartment and called my mother to come pick me up so I could get out. She said she would come later. I wasn't sure if she would come.[1]

> We must not abandon but must deepen our understanding that the problems of families are not merely individual or private. Perhaps [what is] overlooked is our lack of knowledge about the realities of "bad mothers" and their children. (Ashe, 1997, p. 214)

Predispositional factors found to be common to infanticidal mothers include economic stress (Alder & Baker, 1997; Craig, 2004; Doyle & Luckenbill, 1991; Falkov, 1996; Friedman et al., 2005; Ogle, Maier-Katkin, & Bernard, 1996; Smithey, 1997, 2001), family violence, intimate partner violence (Friedman et al. 2005; Smithey 1997, 2001), unplanned pregnancies resulting in unwanted babies (Centers for Disease Control (CDC), 2012; Guttmacher, 2016; Resnick, 1969), lack of family support (Alder & Baker, 1997; Doyle & Luckenbill, 1991; Oberman, 2003; Oberman & Meyer, 2001, 2008) and social isolation (Alder & Baker, 1997; Oberman, 2003; Oberman & Meyer, 2001; Smithey, 1997).

---

[1] Unless otherwise noted, interview data are from my intensives interviews with 14 mothers who killed their infant. The average interview length is 3.1 hours. Most mothers were in a correctional facility at the time of the interviews.

In this chapter, I discuss these predispositions of mothers who have committed infanticide of their biological children as the background circumstances of mother–child interactions. Using data from intensive interviews I conducted with mothers who committed infanticide and data and findings from other studies on infanticide (see appendix for interview guide), I integrate these factors into a social learning and economic deprivation theoretical model to explain how they result in an intensification of childcare. In my work, I stress that these circumstances apply to all mothers in varying degrees, not just those who commit violence against their children: economic inequality and a lack of resources, violence victimization during childhood and intimate partnership, the extent to which the baby was planned and wanted, family support, social isolation, or "going it alone" (Edin & Kefalas, 2005; Hays, 1996; Hochschild, 1997; Lareau, 2003) and substance abuse (Smithey, 1997, 2001). The degree to which these conditions apply to all mothers speaks to the extent to which all mothers are capable of infanticide.

My discussion on the relationship between the economic inequality of women and the ability to mother addresses (1) economic resources for caring for infants such as food, clothing, healthcare, and shelter; (2) stress from the inability to do paid work due to a lack of affordable, quality childcare; and (3) the application of criminological theories of absolute and relative deprivation to these conditions. Next, I discuss experiences and histories of family and intimate partner violence and how they negatively impact the ability to manage stress and interpersonal relations. To these experiences, I apply social learning theory. Then I present research findings on unwanted pregnancy and its impact on parenting, the life-changing event of a birth of a child, and the role social services and extended family play in supporting mothers. I follow with a brief discussion on alcohol use as a coping mechanism. I conclude by integrating the predispositional factors into a model of likelihood of committing infanticide.

2.1.   Economic Inequality and Insufficient Resources

There is a presumption in traditional criminology that experiences of economic hardship are not gendered although the ample research on the gendered allocation of economic resources and the feminization of poverty suggests otherwise. The valid and large amount of research and data on this topic has not been incorporated fully into mainstream criminology to explain female offending, including the commission of homicide. More recently, focus on structural factors such as gender inequality have been found to be related to women's homicide overall (Baron, 1990; Fiala & LaFree, 1988; Jensen, 2001). However, these studies do not distinguish adult from child homicide. This distinction is necessary given the responsibilities, intimacy, and power differences mothers have toward children that are qualitatively different from relationships with adults. The few studies that focus on child homicide (e.g., Alder & Baker, 1997; Crimmins et al., 1997; Oberman, 2003; Oberman & Meyer, 2001; Smithey, 1997, 2001) suggest or imply this distinction. In another work, I quantitatively modeled the common homicide variants of adult homicide – weapon used, age, offender's age, victim's gender, offender's gender, and race/ethnicity – and demonstrate they do not have predictive power when the victim with those parameters will be an infant less than one year of age (Rodriguez & Smithey, 1999). These works on infanticide show that, while a lack of economic resources is important for understanding child homicide, not having needed resources interacts with other social factors producing a much more complex situation, one of which is perceptions of mothers in the workplace.

That women receive significantly lower pay and less opportunity for economic advancement in the workplace is well established. In 2013, female full-time workers had median weekly earnings of US$706, compared to men's median weekly earning of US$860, which is approximately 18% more than women's wages for 2013. This is about a 1% *decrease* in women's pay from a decade earlier. The five-year trend between 2000 and 2005 shows that women averaged 89% of the average full-time pay for men (U. S. Department of Labor, CONSAD Research Corporation, 2016). The Pew Research Center (2016) reports that the average woman is expected to US$430,480 less than the average white man over a lifetime. Currently, women receive 20% less pay than men (National Women's Law Center, 2018). The pay gap is even wider for minorities. Latinas earn 58% of white men's hourly wages, African American women earn 65%, and Asian women earn 87% (Pew Research Center, 2016). Moreover, being poor interacts with the social expectations of childcare. Gurevich's work (2008) finds that "the [childcare] standards themselves, [...] result in disproportionate deviations for poor mothers of color and immigrants, bringing on additional sanctions and hardships" (p. 532).

Women's economic inequality is partly due to cultural inequality and perceptions of mothers. Women who are raising children are expected to put their children "above all else" (Shorter, 1975; Warner, 2005), including economic opportunities and maintaining a wage-paid job (Hays, 1996). Consequently, mothers are paid even less and face more obstacles than women who are not mothers. Mothers earn about 5% less per child than other workers (Budig & England, 2001; Department of Labor, 2017). In addition to managing life with lower pay, the birth of a child is often associated with severe financial strains due to a host of new expenses and restrictions on the ability to earn income (Belsky & Kelly, 1994; Craig, 2004), especially for the lower classes. With the birth of a child and the fulfillment of the expectations of "good" mothering, mothers are believed to be less reliable when workplace and childcare demands compete. Not only is she expected to always choose the care of the child over workplace demands, those who hold this perception condemn mothers who do not give primacy to their children's needs while simultaneously denying or reducing opportunities to advance. Ridgeway (2011) attributes this bias to widely shared cultural schemas about the nature of men and women and finds that a reduction to women's chances of being hired, promoted or receiving a pay raise is based on a combination of the schemas of motherhood and women's status in the workplace. Studies on mommy-tracking, that is, women not advancing in the workplace due to having children or possible pregnancy, show that widely shared cultural beliefs not only categorize working mothers as less competent and committed to workplace responsibilities as compared to non-mothers, but a moral imperative is attached to these beliefs – mothers are culturally expected to be devoted to family while non-mothers and men are expected to be devoted to work (Blair-Loy, 2001). Unfortunately, the consequences of mommy-tracking are self-fulfilling. Wynn (2017) finds that mothers working long hours in the paid labor force perceived themselves according to the culturally unequal expectations of mother and believe that they should devote themselves primarily to caregiving, thereby reducing their own expectation of a higher promotion.

Unpaid labor at home does not fare any better for women in terms of equality than in the paid labor market. The socioeconomic position of women in the United States' capitalist system regarding domestic labor is that it should be unpaid, and thus a "labor of love," and it disproportionately benefits men. Traditionally, men have been expected to provide the primary financial support for families while women have been expected to provide the daily care of the household and children (Hays, 1996; Hochschild, 1989; Lindsey, 2005; Oakley, 1974; Shorter, 1975). This tradition produces gendered, cultural expectations, and gendered identities associated with the importance of gaining and the use of economic resources. For both genders, not having economic resources can provoke chronic frustration that can result in violence (Alder & Baker, 1997; Heimer & Kruttschnitz, 2006; Renzetti, Curran, & Maier, 2012; Smithey, 1997, 2001), albeit for different reasons. Men respond to economic failure as emasculating. Economic success is core to their identity and is the end or the goal. For women, economic success, that is, money, is a means to a different but equally important end: caring for others (Agnew & Broidy, 1997). While postmodern society now expects women to work in the paid labor market in order to have the economic resources necessary for childcare, the expectations of women in the home have changed little (Hays, 1996; Hochschild, 1997). This produces an even greater clash between the two sources of women's inequality – one, increasing demands on time in order to earn sufficient income for family care and, two, unchanged time demands regarding expectations of mothers.

There is a third dimension necessary to understanding the stress of mothering – being a single mother. The stress of house and childcare is even greater for single mothers who must meet the economic goals of both genders to a greater degree by working in the paid labor market and providing the daily care of the household and children without a reliable source of income from a spouse or intimate partner. Child support, when paid, and public assistance are inadequate (Hays, 1996). The reality of receiving childcare subsidies is that they prohibit many single mothers from paid work. The amount received is insufficient to cover childcare costs while working a minimum wage job. Moreover, receiving subsidies and public assistance are heavy-laden with stereotypes of mothers seeking assistance as deviant and failures resulting in a painful, humiliating experience as they try to gain resources for their children (Hays, 1996). These stereotypes only serve to increase the stress of poor, single mothers. And, as previously discussed, when single mothers do paid labor, the social expectations of mothers in the workplace prohibit them from economic advancement which would ease the stress of childcare costs, often keeping them in low-paying jobs.

Without sufficient economic resources, single and middle-to-upper class mothers must work in the paid labor market. This is not a choice and the institutionalization of *mothering* based on a two-parent income operates as though her wage-earning work is a choice and, therefore, the concomitant childcare that allows her to be away from the home for this job, is a choice. Having economic resources to provide for her children is not a choice for poverty and working class mothers and, arguably, is not a choice for middle-class mothers who must meet the appearance of being middle-class, such as nice cars, nice home, and expensive schools and social activities for their children.

The absence of husbands or boyfriends contributes to a mother's economic stress in other ways. Desertion by a husband has three outcomes: emotional loss, economic loss, and increased isolation. Negative changes in a mother's socioeconomic status due to divorce contribute to poorer mental health and greater emotional stress (Lewis & Bunce, 2003; Stroud, 2008) due to lack of assistance and money. For some mothers, the significant outcome of desertion by her intimate partner is homelessness.

Economic resources dictate living conditions and a lack of them often forces extended family and friends to house her and her children to avoid homelessness. This also has adverse effects on the mother's mental health (Kline, 1995), fatigue, and availability of resources from social support networks (Smithey, 1997, 2001). In my interviews with mothers, I find that the living arrangements at the time of the infants' fatal injuries were crowded and the family or friends with whom they were living had become weary of the situation. In these cases, the mother was homeless and had to rely on friends and family for shelter leaving her and her supporters little choice but to endure the situation. They describe the arrangements as small, noisy, no private space, and housing more people than it should. The adverse conditions under which the mothers were living had the potential to exacerbate the stress of infant care. For example:

> I just went by myself, to my friend's house. I was living with my friends. It was a three-bedroom house, I did not have a bedroom, I slept in the living room on the couch and my baby slept in a playpen.

> The house was noisy. [How many people shared the house?][2] Ummm, the mom, two daughters, the son, his wife, four girls and two boys, oh, and (another young mother) and her baby.

---

[2]Brackets denote questions I prompted and parentheses are for the purpose of clarifying meaning or preserving anonymity.

> When the baby was born, we lived with my mom in a three-bedroom house. There were a lot of us there and we kept getting in each other's way.

> The house was small. It had one room. The baby was in a bassinet.

> I was living with friends. They were nice but you could tell they didn't want a baby around.

> I was living with my mom, then I stayed at my grandmother's for a little while, then after I had the baby, I moved back with my mom. It was hard to stay anywhere for too long.

In the following case, the baby's father "dumped" her and the baby on his family.

> We (she and her baby) were living with his uncle, his aunt, his sister, his brother, we were just everywhere (meaning they moved often).

The following interview excerpts depict the environment in which these mothers were attempting to raise their infants as economically deprived conditions resulting in stress as they attempted to live from "day-to-day."

> I knew that I wouldn't be able to meet the financial needs of everything. I couldn't work. Who was gonna take care of the baby?

> Well, I was getting an AFDC check, I was getting food stamps, and sometimes if she ran out of diapers or something like that, my mom would buy diapers, or my grandmother.

> I had worked at McDonald's for two years at minimum wage. When I got pregnant, I went back. I had been working there for six months when my baby died. I had no money. I was living at my mother's house.

> I wanted to get my own house (meaning not having to live with others). They wouldn't let me because I get social services.

Criminological theories support the premise that economic stress is related to violence. Absolute deprivation of economic resources has been linked to violent behavior independent of factors such as race and ethnicity, region of the country, population, or density (Loftin & Parker, 1985). Parker (1989) suggests that violence is one of the few options available to those without the economic resources necessary for everyday living. Depending on how difficult everyday life is for an individual, absolute deprivation may also produce "emotional situations which escalate into violence [...] directed at those close at hand (such as children)" (p. 985).

Economic factors and influences are perhaps the most studied macrolevel factors related to crime. The major premise is that having economic resources is fundamental to all social and cultural structures and that they are a primary force in all bevavioral adjustments to those structures. In a large part, these macro forces determine a person's behavior. Individuals adapt to cultural and economic blockages (Merton, 1938) in several ways, one of which is using violence as an attempt to gain control over the situation (Tittle, 1995). Marx argued that the unequal distribution of wealth in society produces an unequal distribution of power (Marx & Engels, 1988). Powerless individuals have few options for gaining resources and have no power for changing their status in the social contract that dictates their responsibilities and criteria for successfully fulfilling their social roles. Marx argued that "free will," and therefore having control over one's behavior through choices, is not the basis for a lot of behavior. Macro-social structures and power by dominant groups limit or force "choices" on the powerless. He did not see crime as the willful violation of the law or against the common good, but as the "struggle of the isolated individual against the prevailing conditions" (p. 367). Applying these theoretical premises, infanticidal mothers are powerless against their prevailing conditions and, after attempting to manage them, resort to violence as an attempt to gain control over them. In Chapter 5, I discuss the power available to mothers and how the child is the easiest target against which to use it.

For the mothers who were not divorced or had not ended the intimate partnership, long absences from the home by the husband or boyfriend caused her emotional stress and frustration from a lack of assistance with the mundane tasks of caring for the infant (as well as any other children).

> I think he was involved in drugs — he sold them but never used them. He would leave, he stayed lots of places but he was never home. I had the babies all byself to take care of.

> He left all hours of the night. I don't know where he was going or what he was doing. His friends told me he had girlfriends. I don't know. I still don't know.

> Sometimes I would get frustrated because my husband was at work all the time. He said we needed the money but I think he was hanging out with his friends.

> He would never be there with me. Sometimes he would come to sleep and sometimes he'd be gone. Sometimes for two nights. When he did come home, it was 7 or 8 pm and he would eat and go to sleep. Then he would leave the next morning.

In some cases, the infant's father was not living in the home most or all of the time. The consequences of his absence were the same as those described earlier.

> We were in separate houses, I would not see him for days, if I stayed the weekend at his mother's so she could help, we would have a fight. He said I was taking too much of his mother's time. He wouldn't help me but he got mad if she helped me.

> He moved in and out regularly. [How often would he move in and out?] Once or twice a month. [How long would he usually stay when he moved in?] Two or three days, sometimes a couple of weeks.

One mother, whose husband's salary was sufficient for the family's needs, refers to being a stay-at-home mother as being "stuck" at home with little or no leisure time.

> We had money. My husband made over US$70,000. I did not work. My job was (the baby). I was stuck at home all the time. I never got evenings and weekends off.

These stories echo Hochschild's (1989) significant imbalance in leisure time between working husbands and wives and attributes it to the culture of the working mother. For stay-at-home mothers, it may be expected even more so. Women with children in poverty are not stay-at-home mothers by choice but rather are forced into being a stay-at-home mother by a lack of money for paid childcare.

In summary, economic inequality for these mothers resulted in lower resources for goods and buying childcare or hiring babysitters. Many mothers are economically forced to stay at home due to the high cost of childcare. Their work at home is unpaid and they are often overwhelmed. The biological fathers did not contribute economically or with active support in the form of childcare or housework. The absence of the father from the home for frequent and long periods of time reduces support and opportunities for periodic breaks from overwhelming childcare. Divorce makes this situation permanent because the fathers are able to select when and how much they economically contribute and when and for how long they devote time and attention to raising their children. Divorce also increases the likelihood of the mother and children living in poverty and becoming homeless.

2.2.   Family Violence and Intimate Partner Abuse

According to Bandura (1971), behaviors are learned through observation and reinforcement based on environmental and social circumstances. Most behavior is learned through observation, imitation, and reinforcement (Burgess & Akers, 1968; Sutherland & Cressey, 1960). Children do what they see their parents do, even when the modeled behavior does not match what the parents may be telling them to do. The process of observational learning of violence occurs when an individual learns to behave violently by watching another person perform violent actions or by being rewarded for their own use of violent behavior.

The social learning model of violence considers everyday family interactions as precursors to violence (Gelles, 1980). Interactions such as negotiating schedules, attempts to divide housework and childcare, teaching children how to act, or coordinating family activities all have the potential for conflict between parents that can escalate into violence. When parents are violent with each other or toward their children, they are teaching their children to use violence when someone is not doing what they want them to do or to stop doing something they do not want them to do. Family violence research has long held this theory as an explanation for the "cycle of violence" (Gordon, 1988; Widom, 1989). The cycle is the intergenerational transmission of violence in which children learn to be violent by experiencing or witnessing violence from their parents.

Studies on infanticide find that experiencing family violence or intimate partner violence, that is the cycle of violence, is predispositional to infanticide (Bourget & Gagne, 2005; Crimmins et al., 1997; Freidman et al., 2005; Smithey, 1997, 2001; Stroud, 2008). Stroud (2008) describes perpetrators of infanticide as "individuals who had an 'unsettled childhood' [and] a 'disrupted' upbringing due to repeated parent discord [...] (and parental) domestic violence" (pp. 488–489). Crimmins et al. (1997) determined that mothers who killed their children had "damaged selves" from witnessing and experiencing violence as a child.

The mothers in my intensive interviews experienced the cycle of violence and report their parents being physically abusive. The word "beat" is evidence of their perception of the severity of the physical "discipline" they experienced and damage that they continued to experience into adulthood. The mothers use this word to distinguish the physical punishment from a "spanking". For example:

> Sometimes they would spank me, other times they would beat me. [What was the difference between a spanking and a beating?] They would throw me down on the ground and hit me on my head with a fist and I used to see my brothers and sisters get beat down like that too.

> [What would happen if you broke a rule?] Um, well, whenever I broke a rule, um , I'd get spanked by my dad and my mom too. [What were the spankings like?] They would, um, my mom would

> grab my clothes hangers and my dad would, um, hit us with a
> belt or a buckle or anything he could grab. [How many times a
> week would this happen?] A lot when I was growing up, a lot,
> I can't really count the times, I mean I was, used to get beat a lot.

> [Mom] would whup us. She used belts or a switch to beat us.

Parental modeling of violent behavior was often concurrent with direct abuse toward the subject. One mother describes how her father physically abused her mother.

> My mom and dad, they don't get along. [Did your dad and your
> mom ever fight with each other?] Yes they did. [What happened?]
> He would punch her, shove her down. They did a lot of it behind
> closed doors. But we knew what was happening.

Physical violence was not the only form of abuse reported. Some mothers described relations with their parents as emotionally abusive resulting in negative self-feelings.

> I always felt that even when I was doing good, I was doing
> wrong, it was like I never could please them in any way.

> It was more mental abuse than physical. Name-calling. Called
> me 'useless' and 'no good'. My mom was always telling me
> I would never amount to anything. That was mean. Because
> I heard that so long, I started believing it.

Disapproval of the infant's father by the subject's parents often resulted in negative interactional patterns between the subject and the parent.

> Me and my mom, we used to argue all the time 'cause she would
> tell me she didn't like him (the infant's father) 'cause he was
> older than I was. I got tired of her fussing so I told him and we
> moved out.

The cycle of violence is not as deterministic as it sounds. Researchers find that many female victims of child abuse do not grow up to be abusers (Gordon, 1988) and that there are many abusive mothers who were not victims of child abuse (Dougherty, 1993). However, studies suggest that it may have more primacy in infanticide cases where the cycle of violence is clearly evident among the perpetrators and appears to be a significant contributor to infanticides (Alder & Baker, 1997). Experiencing and witnessing violence as a child instilled this response as an option or means of gaining control over another individual, especially one that is seemingly uncontrollable, like a crying baby. These behaviors commonly modeled by parents and subsequently observed by the child, may be more salient than behaviors that have not been frequently modeled or experienced, such as discussion, loss of privileges, time-out, etc. As the mothers become more emotional and distraught, the more familiar behaviors of violence and the internalized message that force gains compliance requires less strategizing and effort than attempts at finding new ways to produce the desired outcome – a not crying baby. The internal, reflective process of choosing among options is discussed extensively in Chapter 4. Another source of violence research finds common to mothers who commit infanticide – intimate partner violence. This too has the effect of modeling violence as a means of control and is emotionally damaging to its victims.

Intimate partner violence is common to many women, not just abusive mothers. According to Archer (2000), studies on intimate partner violence estimate that anywhere from 10% to 35% of the US population will be physically aggressive toward a partner at some point in their lives. The National Coalition Against Domestic Violence (2015) estimates that 33% of women are abused annually with women between the ages of 18 and 24 as the most likely victims. The National Crime Victims Survey (retrieved 2018) data show that 2.2 out of every 1,000 women are victims of intimate partner violence. An estimated two-thirds of female intimate partner violence victimization involved a physical attack, and, from 2002 to 2011, an estimated 50% of these females suffered an injury. A larger percentage of female victims are killed by an intimate partner than male victims (Catalano, 2013). I report these statistics to point out that while my research and that of others find intimate partner violence to be common to infanticidal mothers, it should be taken as a predisposing factor that many women experience. The prevalence of intimate partner violence is common enough that it is safe to assume many women experience it and, consequently, may have the propensity to use violence toward their children.

Beyond being its own predisposing condition, intimate partner violence victimization interacts with economic opportunity and resources. According to the National Coalition Against Domestic Violence (retrieved 2018), victims of intimate partner violence lose a total of eight million days of paid work each year, the equivalent of 32,000 full-time jobs. Between 21% and 60% of victims lose their jobs due to intimate partner violence.

Another consequence of intimate partner violence victimization that precipitates infanticide is suffering and demoralization (to be discussed more extensively in Chapter 3). According to the National Coalition Against Domestic Violence (2015), intimate partner violence victimization is correlated with a higher rate of depression and suicide. In Alder and Baker's (1997) work on maternal filicide (1997), they classify one category as filicide – suicide committed by mothers "who felt that they could not longer cope with the difficult circumstance in which they finds themselves" (p. 28). In four of the seven cases they studied, the women report that their male partner has used physical violence against them. As one of the mothers in their study put it:

> I didn't consider what I was doing was wrong. I just felt I was uniting a family that had suffered a lot [...] I just felt that I have been driven to an absolutely agonizing point where I just couldn't see my way out. (Ronick case, datum cited in Alder & Baker, 1997, p. 27)

Stroud (2008) also finds intimate partner violence to precede infanticide and concludes

> Few (mothers) reports positive and relationships with partners [...] Relationships [with partners] were a source of significant stress [and] lacked practical and emotional support [...] some were socially isolated although not living alone. (p. 495)

Several other studies find similarly that violence victimization by intimate partners is common among mothers who commit infanticide (Bourget & Bradford 2007; Friedman et al., 2005; Stanton & Simpson 2000) including severe physical and sexual assault by different people and partners (Smithey, 1997; Stroud, 2008). Lewis and Bunce (2003) report that in one-third of the mothers they studied, the psychosis believed to precipitate the infanticide was "preceded by severe conflict with the fathers of their children before the filicide event" (p. 463). Jensen's (2001) work on female-perpetrated adult homicide supports this. She concludes that family member homicides "often occur in the context of domestic abuse or other *intense conflict* and when no other solution to a desperate situation can be seen" (p. 2).

Mothers in my study provided detail that describes the infants' fathers as abusive, unsupportive, or antagonistic resulting in emotional stress and, in turn, exacerbated the stress associated with infant care. At a minimum, without being violent or antagonistic toward the mother or children, the intimate partners added to the mother's burden by requiring that she attended to or "mother" them as well. For example:

> It was easier when he wasn't there. I had to cook and clean for him when he was at home. He didn't help with anything − not the house, not the kids, not even himself.
> I was glad that he left. He was more work than the children. And he got angry if I didn't do his stuff first. But I also had to make sure the baby wasn't crying or he would get angry about that. So I got this crying baby on my hip while I am trying to do his stuff.
>
> I needed him to keep giving me money but I didn't want him back in the house. I had enough to do with the baby and all. When he was home, I had to cook and clean for him.

Sherman (2017) studied parenting and also concludes "men experienced lowered self-esteem and a sense of frustration with their relationship dynamics, whereas many women expressed exhaustion with regard to the work of relationships and the burden of caring for a 'childlike' adult" (p. 671).

More than half of the mothers interviewed reported being either legally married to or living with the infants' fathers at the time the infant was killed. Regardless of whether or not the man she was living with was the baby's father, emotional stress stemmed from physical abuse. More than one-half of the subjects report some level and frequency of physical abuse.

> The fights would get as bad as [...] not really bad as far as cutting each other, not like that, he would push, like he would push me into a window and I would cut my hand.

> The same night that he hit me with the vase I went to (the hospital) and I had my son with me at the time and I was trying to tell the police that he did it but he had told me if I told the police, if I did he was going to run off with my son. I didn't have a chance 'cause I was laying up there bleeding in the hospital room and he had my child so I went on and told them that I fell on something which they knew I was lying anyway. So it was basically a lot of fighting, a lot of abuse.

In some cases, the abuse was coupled with isolation due to her abuser prohibiting or reducing her contact with family and friends.

> He was OK for a while, then I started feeling isolated 'cause he was keeping me stuck in the house. He would come home (angry) and take it out on me, you know, beat me. He cut off my friends and tried to cut off my family.

> He started getting jealous, he didn't want me to go around my mom, uh, he didn't want me to be outside, and like he kept me isolated in the house, he had fun, the only time we went out was when he went out and that was just to go over to his mom's house, and, uh, then the beatings started, maybe three months later.

Another mother related how, although her husband was never physically abusive, his constant negative evaluations of her as a wife resulted in emotional stress.

> We're military, my husband is a sort of high-ranking army officer and I could no longer live up to his perfect mold of a wife. [Did

you tell him this?] No. [What kept you from telling him?] I don't know. I tried to be perfect and telling him sounded imperfect.

While not all mothers reported relationships with the baby's father as physically abusive, they all described the father as unsupportive or antagonistic. Unsupportive fathers were either ignoring or "clueless" about the amount of chronic, detailed care required when raising a child or they overtly refused to help.

The social learning predispositional factors previously described, present a parent who experienced undue emotional stress from her interpersonal relationships with her primary socialization agents, that is, her parents, and individuals with whom she attempted to create a new primary group, that is, her nuclear family. This stress is exacerbated by whether the pregnancy was planned, how much the baby was wanted, and the reality of parenting.

2.3. Unwanted Pregnancy and the Reality of Parenting

The conception of a child happens under varying circumstances that can range from wanting and planning a child to an unplanned, unwanted pregnancy. Planning strongly suggests wanting a child. Current data show that most pregnancies are planned or welcomed (CDC, 2012) at fairly specific times in a mother's life, such after having a job for a specified period of time, getting a sought-after promotion, or earning a certain level of income. Due to medical advancements, both involving birth control and fertility techniques, mothers have more options for control when she gets pregnant. As a result, the trend over the past decade shows an overall, substantial decrease in unwanted pregnancies.

However, there are still a significant number of unplanned pregnancies. Anywhere from one-third (CDC, 2012) to almost one-half (Guttmacher Institute, 2016) of pregnancies are unplanned or unintended. In one of my ongoing research projects, I collect quantitative data on expectations of parenting. Of 208 parents in this study thus far, 68% report the last pregnancy was unplanned (Smithey, 2018). The Guttmacher Institute report on unintended pregnancy states that 45% of all pregnancies are either unwanted or mistimed, meaning the mother wanted to eventually have children but at a later date. "Mistimed" implies that the mother believes her current circumstances are not conducive to the time and resources needed for childrearing. She could also be fulfilling a career goal that, once complete, would better situate her for the home—workplace time demands.

About one-half of unintended pregnancies are terminated (Guttmacher Institute, 2016). This is a small increase over a decade ago. There are many reasons women with unintended pregnancies do not get abortions, mainly a lack of money to pay for it, religious beliefs, and a fear of informing someone about the pregnancy, including denying the pregnancy to herself.

An unplanned pregnancy does not necessarily mean the child is unwanted. Children from unplanned pregnancies can be placed on a continuum of very much wanted to very much unwanted. However, there is a very plausible relationship between unwanted children and the likelihood of violence toward that child or any other children the mother is raising. Barber, Axinn, and Thornton (1999) studied unwanted childbearing and find that some unwanted children become wanted by the time they are born. They find also that "mothers with unwanted births [...] are substantially more depressed and less happy than mothers without unwanted births" and that these mothers report "spanking and slapping their children more" than mothers who wanted the baby by the time is was born (p. 252). They conclude that the negative consequences for children born from unwanted pregnancies are more serious than for children who were wanted or even just mistimed. Other studies support the hypothesis that a child being unwanted can increase the chances of violence toward it or other children (Mugavin, 2005; Stroud, 2008). I discuss unwanted babies and the escalation of violence toward the children more extensively in Chapter 4.

My intensive interview data from mothers who killed their infant show that some of the pregnancies were unwanted for different reasons. Statements such as "it was a bad situation," "I didn't want to get pregnant," and "I did not want another baby" demonstrate the unwantedness of the infant.

> Becoming pregnant was a bad situation for me. I wasn't married. No one helped me because I have a baby. No one wanted to do anything with me.

> I didn't really want to get pregnant, I wasn't ready for it. When I found out that I was pregnant, it shocked me 'cause at first I didn't want to have kids. I wasn't ready and I know it was going to be hard for me because I was living with friends. I really did not want kids.

> I did not want another baby. I had my little girl and it was all I could do to take care of her and the house (she lived in military housing with strict rules).

> My social worker said I had no psychological bond with my baby. I guess that's true. I didn't want to fool with it. I hadn't planned on having it.

In one case, the mother wanted family to adopt her child but they told her to get an abortion instead. Her religion affected her decision to not have an abortion.

> At first I didn't know what to do, I was confused, okay, so I decided to keep it, and I was going to give it to my aunt and uncle. But later my aunt told me I should get an abortion and my

uncle was mean about it. So then I was going to give custody to my friend's mom, but she had a drinking problem. [Did you consider an abortion?] I did not consider an abortion at all. I was Catholic, but not anymore. Now I am nothing (regarding religious affiliation).

In another case, the mother wanted to terminate the pregnancy but her personal physician discouraged her and she was afraid to enter a clinic.

I asked my doctor about getting an abortion but he encouraged me to have the baby. I checked on abortion clinics but there were protests and I was afraid of being hassled. I asked my mom about it and she was against it and told me to get my tubes tied.

The stress and consequences of managing a pregnancy may result from the biological father's lack of desire to have children. In two cases, the baby's father did not want the baby.

(My boyfriend) hated the idea that I was pregnant. After the baby was born, he was just real quiet.

When I told (the baby's father) I was pregnant, he wanted me to have an abortion. I wanted the baby.

In two cases, the father denied paternity as a means to alleviate responsibility for the child and emotionally abuse the mother.

When I told him (her common law husband) I was pregnant with his baby, he said "no, it is someone else's baby". I couldn't believe it and cried for days. I was never with anyone else.

Well, for a while he (the biological father) was all right. Then he started denying her, he would way she wasn't his so we would get into arguments and he would say "that's not my little girl". He'd just say that 'cause he didn't want to fool with her. He'd say that my oldest son was his and my little girl wasn't.

None of the mothers had planned to get pregnant. There were mothers who wanted their unplanned child, at least while they were pregnant, and used the word "happy" to describe their condition.

I was happy about being pregnant. It was something I wanted.

I was very happy; I wanted a little baby you know, especially one of my own.

Stroud (2008), who also studied infanticidal mothers, described the "unlooked-for birth as a source of difficulty and stress [...] ambivalent and negative attitudes toward the child were reported." (p. 498). She reports that some of the mothers essentially rejected their child and "gave accounts of feelings of panic, despair, and isolation immediately before the offence. None had any history of mental illness and were described by witnesses as 'nice people'" (p. 494).

But a wanted baby can become unwanted or less wanted due to the reality of parenting. Mugavin (2005) studied infanticide and, in one case, finds that "the victim [...] was *no longer* wanted" (p. 66), implying that the baby was wanted at some time before the murder. This finding addresses how even a wanted child can become unwanted due to the mother's lack of preparedness and beforehand knowledge of the demands of childcare, especially newborn care. Maushart (1999), who researched the reality of parenting, aptly describes this disjuncture as "cultural schizophrenia". She states, "The gap between image (i.e., romanticized parenting) and reality, between what (mothers) show and what (they) feel, has resulted in a peculiar cultural schizophrenia about motherhood" (p. 9), and that "we, as a society, fail to anticipate the depth and breadth of the mothering experience" (p. 10). It seems also that not only does society fail to fully socialize women into the realities of mothering and thus better prepare them, society may be complicit in infanticide by coercing women to reproduce by romanticizing marriage and having children. Rossiter (1988) who conducted an intensive study into the transition into motherhood finds emergent themes from her interview data to be "Shock," "Being Unprepared," "Panic," "Anxiety," "Not Knowing," and "Feeling Out of Control." Or as Ashe (1997) puts it, "there is nothing like the responsibility of caring for children to remind parents of our limitations" (p. 210).

Moreover, the cultural norms and history of unrealistic expectations of childbearing is so entrenched in both men and women that it would be very difficult to overtly change if society were to attempt to do so. Maushart (1999) points out that "to the one being socialized into the romanticized beliefs about being a mother, revealing the truth would be 'news' [...] and might not be believed by women anyway" (p. 5).

The entrenchment and inability to make women and men aware of the unrealistic expectations of mothers is because romanticized socialization of marriage and bearing children upholds patriarchal society. The history of gender roles can be summed up by the old phrase that women are supposed to "be barefoot and pregnant." Bearing children has long been a form of oppression experienced by women. My contention that coercing women into marriage and having children upholds patriarchy is supported by work on women in the workplace (previously discussed), the inequality of women at home (discussed in the next chapter), and the entrapment women experience once they become mothers (discussed in Chapter 5). A woman staying at home and bearing children without the resources to do so not only subjugates her, it puts her child at risk of violence. Sick, tired, and unwell babies cry. As Wall (2001) finds in his research on infanticidal mothers, "[many mothers] 'talk [...] of feeling inadequate in the face of a continually crying baby and of a loss of personal identity as their whole world becomes centered on a baby" (p. 598). The centering may not necessarily be due

Table 2.1. Planned Pregnancy, Wanted Baby, and Likelihood of Lethal Injury.

	Wanted Baby	**Unwanted Baby**
Planned	Lowest likelihood of lethal injury	Moderate-to-high likelihood of lethal injury
Unplanned	Moderate-to-low likelihood of lethal injury	Highest likelihood of lethal injury

to unwantedness but may be due to the invasion or imposition of the baby into daily life and the realization that there are many economic and cultural barriers that prevent them from continuing the life they had before becoming mothers.

Furthermore, caring for unwanted babies can transcend generations if the mother herself was an unwanted baby. Work by Barber et al. (1999) finds that mothers with unwanted births share less affection with those children. How wanted the mother was by her parents can result in lower levels of extended family support due to lessened affection in a cyclical manner – parents of an adult mother are less likely to care for the mother's child if they did not have strong feelings for her when she was a baby. Consequently, unwantedness of herself and her baby by the mother's parents can affect how likely she is to ask them for help.

How planned and how wanted the baby produces different levels of likelihood of lethal injury. I argue in Chapters 4 and 5 how unwantedness can contribute to a mother's heightened emotion that can result in a higher likelihood of inflicting a lethal injury as her unwantedness of the baby fuels her rage as she assaults her child.

As background, I model the effect of how planned and wanted a child is on injury into four possibilities in Table 2.1.

Based on this model, the violent episodes for the unplanned, unwanted babies take on a dimension of instrumental violence due to a subconscious desire to eliminate the problem. In fact, classifications of child abuse and homicide often include the instrumental act of eliminating an unwanted child (e.g., d'Orban, 1979).

2.4.   Social Isolation and Family Support

Another important predisposing factor in infanticide is social isolation stemming from a lack of social and extended family support (Bourget & Gagne, 2005; Friedman et al., 2005; Oberman, 2003; Oberman & Meyer, 2001, 2008; Smithey, 1997, 2001; Stanton, Simpson, & Wouldes, 2000). Such support reduces the emotional stress, fatigue, and loss of sense of self many mothers experience. Support from family and friends can provide knowledge about child rearing from their own experiences and can help struggling mothers craft a new course of action. If nothing else, it can give her a much-needed break to restore her mental and physical reserves. Oberman and Meyer (2001) studied mothers who kill their children and concludes that "[infanticide does] not occur solely because of a mother's mental impairment. Rather it results from a combination of the mother's vulnerable mental status and the social isolation and other pre-dispositional factors that shape the context in which she is expected to parent" (p. 175).

Similarly, Stanton et al. (2000) find "[infanticide] deaths occurred in a context of psychosocial stress and limited support." Both of theses studies indicate that if the mother had more access to familial, friend, and social support, the risk of infanticide would have been reduced. However, I must note that there is a down-side to formal social support, which is criminalizing "bad" mothering. The increased surveillance of mother by the courts and social services contribute to their stress. I discuss this more thoroughly in the next chapter.

Extended families are the primary source of support for most mothers and may serve to reduce a mother's stress. Most family members have emotional attachments to grandchildren, nieces, and nephews and want to spend time with them. They offer to babysit when needed. But in some cases I studied, there was little, no, or only temporary support. A few of the mothers in my study did not have parents or a close enough relationship with their parents and siblings to receive or ask for help. In these cases, the mother's family members were unwill-ing or unable to assist with caring for the infant. For example:

> I was not close enough to anyone in my family to talk to about problems.

> My mother left when I was 12. Then I was in foster care and chil-dren's shelters until I was 18. I never really had parents.

> I was adopted. Then my adoptive parents divorced. My mom remarried. I don't see her much. My dad was hurt in a car wreck; he has head injuries and lives in a nursing home. He can't help me.

> Mom was very understanding. She would try to be there for me, but she was already raising my sister's kids. I couldn't really ask her to take care of my kids too.

With limited or no resources to periodically escape her stressful situation, mothers were left to develop their own means of coping.

> Even before things happened, I asked my own family for help and they turned me down. My father had a lot of things to work out for himself. He had a drinking problem. He would get blitzed on the weekends. I don't have much contact with my mom. Her and my father separated and that really broke the ties. I was in high school. I really thought that my dad back then (when she was younger) never wanted to spend any time with us kids.

> They would help, [...] really it depends on when I needed to go
> somewhere. This was so I could rest. Or they'd go shopping for
> me. But this only lasted about a couple of months. Then they was
> tired of it all.

Part of the social isolation the mothers experienced was from the biological
father's absence. In one case, the father returned to work one week after the
birth. The mother attributed this to not much interest in the baby.

> He was helpful the first week the baby was home. Then he went
> back to work. Then it was all on me. He was not upset when he
> found out our baby was dead.

In another case, the mother claimed the father had very little attachment and
stated that he didn't hold the baby a lot. She saw this as a lack of interest in the
child and in being a father. Another case of help from the husband was
described as counter-productive parenting practices that lead to him reducing
his help with the children.

> My husband didn't help me and he was too lenient with our (four)
> children. He didn't want to make them behave so he just quit.

Some parents of the mother did not like the biological father and this reduced
help and support from both sides.

> My family didn't like my husband. He knew it. He didn't want to
> be around them and told me to stay home with the kids so he
> could be home with them. He just wanted them (her parents) to
> know they were his kids and it was up to him if they saw them.
> But then I was stuck feeding and chasing kids because he
> wouldn't do it.

> My mom didn't like my boyfriend. It was real uncomfortable.
> I just quit going over there if (her boyfriend) was with me.

The predisposing factors interact in a serial manner to paint a more complex
situated context in which infanticide occurs. Ogle et al. (1996) describe the necessary conditions for violence toward children as they are related to the predisposing factors faced by the perpetrator as a combination of events: a crisis causing
increased stress, actual or perceived lack of support, and perceived shortcoming
in the victim. They argue that these combined predispositions are sources of
chronic high arousal, especially among those in absolute poverty, and result in
explosions of angry aggression against visible and vulnerable targets. For
marginalized groups, such as minorities and immigrants, the social isolation
interacts with economic deprivation, insecurity due to powerlessness over their

environment, social status as a minority, and decreased opportunity to gain needed resources including social services (Brown & Kennelly, 1999). Even more than women citizens, immigrant mothers have stressful lives with disappoint-ment of employment hopes, little or no economic resources, fear of deportation, and language difficulties (Stroud, 2008).

From my research and that of others, I find the situated context of infanti-cide is even more complex than the predispositions discussed in this chapter. This multifaceted source of stress and suffering causes chronic, high arousal that leads to a breakdown in reality and mental wellness. In the remainder of this book, I argue that the cultural expectations of mothering interact with inadequate resources to fulfill them. Being a victim of child abuse and intimate partner violence, ending up with an unplanned, unwanted pregnancy, and having little or no social support, have the highest likelihood of committing infanticide. I diagram the pathways to infanticide that these conditions produce in Figure 2.1.

The diagram presented in Figure 2.1 is based on the theoretical premise that my work and the work of others suggest – that the predisposing factors described in this chapter affect the chances of a mother committing infanticide. Mothers who have a planned pregnancy resulting in a baby that remains wanted, have sufficient economic resources, and are supported by their family, both extended and the baby's father, are the least likely to commit infanticide. Inversely, mothers who experience the chronic stressors of an unplanned, unwanted baby that is being raised with insufficient economic resources, and has little or no family support are the most likely to commit infanticide. While it

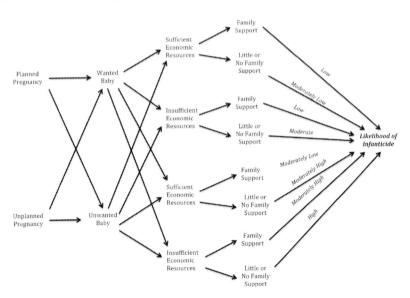

Figure 2.1. Predispositional Factors and the Likelihood of Maternal Infanticide.

may be tempting to draw the line between violence and no violence toward the baby or between child abuse and homicide as a way to separate abusive mothers from nonabusive mothers, I contend that all mothers experience these conditions in varying degrees. The presumption that those who have resources will always have resources, and those who have support will always have support is misguided and keeps women off-guard, potentially resulting in an underestimation of how she may act under chronic, demoralizing, and stressful circumstances. The temptation to believe that only poor or mentally ill women could harm their children fails to account for the power of social circumstances. The model presented is a complex continuum of this power with several pathways, on which any mother could potentially find herself.

In summary, my research and that of others find that when infant homicide occurred at the hands of the mothers studied, it was the result of a culmination of predisposal factors evolving from the mothers' socialization experience and precipitating factors stemming from economic deprivation and a lack of interpersonal support. The socialization of these mothers is characterized by abuse or trauma from relatives as well as physically abusive intimate partner relationships. These mothers not only had little or no emotional support, but the relationships they had with others tended to be emotionally destructive. The biological fathers of the infants were abusive, emotionally unsupportive, or antagonistic. These fathers played a minimal role, if any, in economic support thus leaving the unskilled mothers to garner their own resources for survival while simultaneously raising children.

These common social conditions under which women are expected to raise their children constitute a form of societal coercion and violence toward women. Moreover, given the intangible nature of the expectations and social conditions, mothers have no clear target against which to defend herself. Consequently, children become the vulnerable targets of lethal injury due to these predispositional factors and conditions under which society, aggressively and punitively, expects women to meet the social expectations of mothering (Bernard, 1990; Hays, 1996; Steele, 1987). This is a glaring form of cultural inequality against women. These oppressive, prohibitive conditions are socially constructed and institutionalized and negatively affect a women's ability to meet the larger social expectations and definitions of the mothering ideology of what constitutes "good mothering."

Chapter 3

Cultural Inequality and the Mothering Ideology

So there I was. No money. No formula and out of diapers. Her daddy was never around and when he did come around, it was because he had spent his paycheck and was hungry. He said taking care of the babies is my job. We have two babies. I had a minimum wage job but I lost it because my littlest one got sick and I had to stay home with her. Then I couldn't pay the daycare anymore. So I had both babies at home with me. She cried because she was hungry and wet. I had stretched the last few diapers as far as I could because I knew I couldn't get more until the end of the next week. She got a rash.

This story encapsulates a history of gender socialization and societal expectations that have produced cultural inequality by placing a much lower value on women's work than men's work – both in the paid labor force of the economic social institution and in the unpaid labor force at home (Crittenden, 2001; Hays, 1996; Hochschild, 1989, 1997; Oakley, 1974a, 1974b). In both social institutions, women are expected to do more while being rewarded less. The ideology of mothering is a major cultural inequality that limits women's ability to gain reward and participate on equal terms with men in the paid work force and at home. This limitation contributes to the devaluation of women's paid work, childcare, and household care.

In this chapter, I discuss the division of labor in the home and the cultural inequality of excessive demand on women to achieve "good mothering." I present the work of other sociologists who find that mothering is unrealistically labor-intensive and that women are required to fulfill the "second shift" of household and childcare (Hays, 1996; Hochschild, 1989).

Furthermore, cultural inequality at home and work, the middle-class standard of "good" mothering, and the child-rearing industry are significant social forces that shape the mother identity and maintain the lack of power mothers have to change institutionalized, societal expectations in both spheres. Under these conditions, mothers are expected to raise their children in their spare time and with their spare change as the workforce mandates long workdays with low pay. Moreover, the criminal justice system and social services enforce the mothering ideology and the conditions under which women must fulfill it by criminalizing "poor" mothering. I argue that these conditions of cultural and economic inequality are foundational to the mandated, social expectations of mothering and are culturally reproduced predispositions to violence by mothers toward their infants. Due to excessive social and economic strain to meet expectations of the mothering ideology, these conditions of inequality contribute to lethal injuries of infants.

3.1. Cultural Inequality and the Devaluing of Mothering: Raising Your Children in Your Spare Time and with Your Spare Change

Historically, men have been expected to provide the primary financial support for families while women have been expected to provide the daily care of household and children (Hays, 1996; Oakley, 1974a,1974b). These gendered expectations produce and reproduce cultural inequality at home and in the workplace and serve to keep mothering and other types of women's work devalued. Women have always been expected to bear and raise children. Men have not been held to this expectation. All other social institutions uphold this inequality and filter roles and achievements of mothers through it. The cultural inequality of women's work is exacerbated by pervasive, gendered economic inequality. The ideology of mothering has limited women's ability to participate in the workforce on equal terms with men and contributed to the devaluation of women's paid work, childcare, and domestic labor (Kline, 1995). As discussed in Chapter 2, women receive significantly lower pay than men and lessened opportunity for economic advancement in the workplace. Mothers who work in the paid labor force experience the strain of balancing work and family. They are expected to work full time and strive for resources while meeting the cultural mothering expectation of working a "second shift of an extra twenty-four hours a month each year" (Hochschild, 1989, p. 3). Analyzing time diaries of mothers, Bianchi, Robinson, and Milkie (2006) find that fathers tend to work 21 hours a week of childcare and housework and mothers tended to work 41 hours a week. They point out further that when considering that both worked about 65 hours a week in the paid labor market, mothers have very little time for themselves. Kalil and Ziol-Guest (2013), find similar results when analyzing the Time Use Survey (Department of Labor [DOL], 2013) from 2007 through 2011. Fathers, on average, spend 82.82 minutes daily on house care and 53.33 minutes daily on childcare. Mothers spend almost double those amounts with 159.59 minutes on house care and 102.28 minutes on childcare.

Due to this devaluation, the social institutions of economics and family are often in conflict. Job security for women is tenuous due to "mommy-tracking" and frequent interruptions in women's work schedules to attend to the culturally expected childcare demands (Hays, 1996; Hochschild, 1997; Sutherland, 2010). The expectation that mothers must put their children ahead of their jobs is part of intensive mothering and creates what Hays (1996) calls the cultural contradiction of motherhood: women must achieve economically but must also attend to the children. Mothers must demonstrate their children are their priority or else be deemed "bad mothers."

There is no leniency in failing to meet the cultural expectations of mothering. Such leniency would reduce the significant strain caused by the cultural contradiction. It does not matter what her economic aspirations — career or just paying the bills — a good mother must attend to her children first regardless of how overwhelming and unrealistic the expectations. Hochschild (1989) makes a similar conclusion and argues that marriages are stuck in a stalled revolution. The expectations of women in the workplace have not been met with a reduction of the expectations of work at home. This is particularly true for childcare. More recently, Sayer, Bianchi, and Robins (2004) find similarly that the ideals of good mothering have broadened to include accepting that she is a wage earner, but mothers have not been released from the normative expectations that they will devote all their time and resources to child-rearing. Consequently, the vast majority of women *must work* and *must be good mothers* all the while society is not adjusting the amount of social support provided or changing the expectations of either social institution. The larger portion of the day must be spent earning money but the amount of time at home and the money earned are insufficient for meeting the expectations of raising children. There are frequent, unexpected expenses that can only be covered with "spare change." This structural and cultural conflict produces suffering mothers who are more likely to commit violence toward child. Sometimes the violence is lethal.

The recognition of the stalled revolution and lack of adjustment for the contradictory cultural requirements of work versus family is obscured by belief in maternal attachment. Part of the ideology of mothering is that it is instinctual and a natural bond occurs automatically for every mother. This belief is socially constructed as a means to control women and nature is often used as a way to gain acceptance of a cultural construct. Cronon (1995) argues the same and concludes "[...] for those who wish to ground their moral vision in external reality [...] [nature has the] capacity to take disputed values and make them seem innate, essential, eternal, and nonnegotiable" (p. 36). Eyer (1993) similarly explains that during the postnatal period, women are hormonally influenced to be more or less accepting of a newborn and suggests that "the zeal with which (natural) bonding was accepted (in science and lay society)" is explained by the fact that it fit within "a deeply embedded ideology regarding the proper role of women" (pp. 8–9). Consequently, society at large and many mothers uphold belief in "natural," maternal attachment.

However, history does not fully support this belief. Shorter (1975) argues that belief in maternal attachment began with industrialization and that mothers do not automatically attach to a child due to gestation and birth. Rather, mothers attach to children due to romantic love of intimate partners. With industrialization, young men and women had the option of working in factories thereby forgoing the control of their father over their future wealth. This social arrangement unseated arranged marriages and created a social space for marriage based on romantic love. The love felt for the children of this union is an extension of that romantic love. Hays (1996) also questions maternal attachment and maintains that early perceptions of infants were of underdeveloped, sometimes demonic beings who had not yet become "human" and were therefore not automatically "loveable." Eventually, the social constructs of childhood and loving parents were heavily influenced by the pre-twentieth century traditional parenting practices (which also varied chronologically depending on social class) including attachment due to maternal instinct. This is debated in sociohistorical research but the impact of belief in attachment, regardless whether it is a social construct or natural state, has serious consequences for mothering in modern and postmodern society.

One common consequence is that working women with children or mothers who do not always have positive feelings toward their children experience guilt (Hays, 1996; Smithey, 1997) because they believe they should naturally, always feel such love toward their child that they want nothing else. The strain and guilt are due to the content of the ideology of intensive mothering and child-rearing "expertise," not by being unnatural mothers. The ideology does not allow for time away from their child or negative feelings toward their child. Mothers who look forward to work as a means of escaping childcare or who do not like or have positive feelings toward all their children, feel guilty and believe they are being "bad" mothers and do not readily share these feelings with others. This makes social isolation even more likely and problematic. Those who do not like interacting with them or resent the work of care, must stage a different front – a happy mother who knows how to keep her children healthy and happy. How well she fronts this image directly impacts her self-image.

Ogle, Maier-Katkin, and Bernard (1996) argue further that there is a difference by men and women in the coping mechanisms and management of self-image. Women evaluate their self-worth based on the value and success of interpersonal relationships, and despair and failure resulting in anger involves alienation from those very relationships. This leads women to cognitively reinterpret situations to preserve relationships (Broidy & Agnew, 1997; Lerner, 1980). The goal of the reinterpretation is to delegitimize their anger and resentment and recast it as guilt.

A mother's ability to stage a happy front and fulfill her expectations of the good mother identity is made salient when she interacts with her infant. The child is a significant symbol whose state of being at any moment is a reflection of her agency as a mother and her success in face of the expert-driven requirements of "good mothering."

3.2.   The Guardians of the "Stock of Knowledge" and the Child-rearing Industry

Potential actors of institutionalized actions must be educated to the meanings and experts provide the knowledge (Berger & Luckmann, 1966). For women, this education consists of primary and secondary socialization. Primary socialization includes nurturing and caring about others. Women are taught to value interpersonal relationships and to give high priority to the feelings of others. Secondary socialization instills the values, goals, and beliefs of a specialized role, such as being a "good" mother. This learned content constitutes the expectations used by mothers and others to judge how well she is fulfilling the role. For the mothering role, there has been a significant influence by "experts" who define the expectations of specialized roles, have the power to create new expectations, and have the power to institutionalize the methods for meeting them. The learned content of the social expectations of being a woman and a mother becomes a frame of reference or practical consciousness (Giddens, 1979) — that as we are socialized, we gain tacit stocks of knowledge from which we draw as we constitute social activity. Berger and Luckmann (1966) refer to this constitution as "social construction" as we use the content interactively. The degree to which we use this discursive consciousness varies according to the amount it penetrates (Giddens, 1979) or has become internalized via socialization (Berger & Luckmann, 1967). The mothering ideology is "learned as objective truth in the course of socialization and thus internalized as subjective reality" (Berger, 1966, p. 66). This reality in turn has power to shape the individual. The reality of mothering or the mothering ideology will produce a specific type of person whose identity and biography as a mother have meaning only in a universe constituted by the body of knowledge […] that has been socially produced and objectivated with reference to this activity. To "be a mother" implies existence in a social world defined and controlled by the body of knowledge known as "mothering."

The mothering ideology consists of cultural schemas that construct the social institution of the family, especially the gendering of parenting which creates cultural inequality. These schemas are embedded in a mother's intellect as a "stock of knowledge" of mothering that is socially produced and found in valid descriptions of everyday life. Mothers comparing themselves to their own mothers, mothers portrayed in the media, or mothering instructions from experts (such as doctors, social service agents, authors, etc.) validates the descriptions. These descriptions and the validity of the knowledge based in belief or claims constituted in the discourse of experts form a mothering ideology that constrains mothers to a lower social place, both relative to social class and men. Ideologies have the capability of dominant groups or classes to make their own sectional interests appear to others as universal or natural (Giddens, 1979, 1984), as is the case of belief in "maternal instinct." They are a resource for the dominant cultural group. The "valid" portrayals of "good" mothering are often selected according to the beliefs of the more powerful groups. The ideology, regardless of whether it fits the reality of the social groups to which the mother belongs, becomes internalized normative imperatives. This dynamically sustains and changes social structure but the change is beyond the agency of one person. Consequently, mothers have no choice but to strive to meet the unrealistic social imperatives.

Furthermore, the mothering ideology demands fulfillment of the very important social function of social reproduction while not expecting societal support. Given the economic resources needed to raise children, American culture requires that parents raise children with their spare change and in their spare time and the crux of this unrealistic task falls to women. Hays (1996) captures the strain and importance of mothering as producing "intensive mothering" where women are mandated to meet the cultural responsibility for social reproduction within the situational context of taking for granted a cultural model of natural, intensive, self-sacrificing, and isolated motherhood. The mandate is that childcare must be done by the mother, must be labor-intensive, and is beyond a market value. The full scope of the ideology work is a measure of the power of the stress experienced by American mothers today. And the experience is relentless. Regardless of what we have learned about mothering, the expectations do not subside, must be achieved, and mothers must strategize continuously about how to live up to the unrealistic state of affairs that that constructed mothering. As Hays (1996) concludes, "These stresses and the strain toward compensatory strategies should actually be taken as a measure of the persistent strength of the ideology of intensive mothering" (p. 75) that represents a "symbolic universe" for legitimating one's social position and moral correctness in taking the role. Based on the "moral fitness" of the mother and the extent to which she is achieving the role, it reinforces who is considered a good or bad mother. Paraphrasing Berger:

> The symbolic universe orders and thereby legitimates everyday roles, priorities, and operating procedures by placing them in the context of the most general frame of reference conceivable. [...] To be a [parent or other status] is legitimated as a mode of being in the symbolic universe − it is conducive to feelings of security and belonging. The individual can assure [him or herself] that [she or he] is living "correctly". The correctness of his life is legitimated on the highest level of generality. (1966, p. 9)

The symbolic universe, or stock of knowledge, orders or prioritizes the world into objects that are apprehended as "reality" based in tradition. For the reality of mothering, a crying baby must be assuaged to meet the high priority of a happy, healthy baby. The sources of the mothering information order and legitimate the priority of the role of mother. This knowledge serves as a "[...] controlling force in itself, an indispensable ingredient of the institutionalized, expected conduct. Fulfilling the expected conduct is a means for inclusion in the larger culture" (Berger & Berger, 1972, p. 58). In other words, meeting the priorities of the institutionalized information of the mothering ideology, allows a mother to believe she belongs to the larger society. She perceives herself as being capable and accepted by others. If she is unsuccessful, she believes she must strive toward capability to gain acceptance. But her lack of success is not necessarily a result of her own inability to meet the social imperatives, but rather due to the rigidity of what is deemed "successful." The stock of knowledge is intergenerationally transmitted, thereby sustaining the institutionalized process and creating history. With each generation, the interactional patterns harden or thicken. The expected actions come to exist beyond the mother and possess a reality of their own. This reality confronts the mother as an external and coercive fact. In this case, the coercive fact is that good mothers have happy babies. And, when achieved, this sense of success and belonging lasts only until the next time the baby cries.

But meeting the priorities and therefore "living correctly" is nearly impossible when the content for good mothering is in unclear, contradictory state partly due to the capitalistic, competitive child-rearing industry. I discuss later in this chapter how this industry plays a prominent role in the production of the content of the mothering ideology. Mothers are unable to evaluate their own stock of knowledge due to the sheer number of conflicting expectations generated by this industry. Consequently, mothers, often with direction from others such as social services, doctors, and criminal justice personnel, turn to "experts" who are generally available via media, books, sometimes mandate parenting classes, and other formats.

3.3. "Good" Mothering: A Middle-class Standard

The knowledge of mothering is a stock of information transmitted through discourse. The currently overwhelming and disorganized nature of the content is contradictory and produces negative self-judgments but remains the source for definitions of "right" and "wrong" for the mother. This discourse serves as a socially organizing belief system of what constitutes a good mother regardless of how socially disorganized the actual content. But perhaps more problematic than the onslaught of conflicting, untested information on how to mother, the ideology assumes mothers have automatic attachment to their children and sufficient resources to raise them. This imposes dominant, middle-class cultural values and childcare practices on all mothers regardless of social class. In her work on cultural contradictions of motherhood, Hays (1996) concludes the discourse about motherhood is shaped by the white, middle-class ideology of intensive mothering. This standard and the assumptions of automatic attachment and sufficient resources devalue further the lower- and working-class cultural values and parenting practices. For women without the resources or time to live up to the middle-class standards of mothering, the ideology is unrealistic and the expectations these women hold for themselves are self-defeating. This creates a duality as mothering is central to the lives of lower-class women regardless of race/ethnicity, because children provide stability and meaning more so than marriage or cohabitation (Collins, 1991; Edin & Kefalas, 2005). Motherhood has been ideologically constructed for those women considered "fit" and women have often been judged "unfit" on the basis of their social class. When mothers are considered to be unfit due to social position rather than behavior, it is difficult, if not impossible, for them to meet the societal image of the "good mother" identity (Kline, 1995) and cope with the powerful constraints of the social institution of parenting.

Hays (1996) argues further that middle-class women are, in some respects, "those who go about the task of child-rearing with the greatest intensity." While Hays is correct about child rearing may be a greater focus, middle-class women do not face the greatest *challenge* nor experience the greatest despair – poverty-class mothers do. The mothering ideology is an impossible list to accomplish even for middle-class women, the social class standard by which all mothers are judged, but for lower- and poverty-class mothers, it is even more impossible to meet. Besides the lack of time and resources, lower-class mothers are subjected to greater scrutiny by social services and the criminal justice system, and, when found in violation of "good mothering" norms, they lack the resources to effectively challenge this finding and subsequent sanctions.

3.4.   The Mother Identity and the Power of Institutionalized Behavior

At the center of this context of the disorganized ideology, class dominance, and cultural and economic inequality is the identity of "mother." The identity is so core to a mother that the word "mother" becomes her master status regardless of whether she wants it to be. It becomes "who she is, who she feels herself to be, and is deeply gender-based" (Rothman, 2000, p. 155). There is a difference between "mother" and the "mother identity." *Mother* is a label given to a person who is biologically or legally fulfilling the role of raising a child. A *mother identity* is internalized and embraced to varying degrees by women who take on the mothering role.

The mother identity becomes internalized and sustained through gender socialization during which people are educated into a role by rewarding and punishing their behavior (Bandura, 1965). The emphasis placed during this education creates core identities (McCall & Simmons, 1966; Nuttbrock & Freudiger, 1991; Stryker, 1968). The expectations of the mother identity become routinely awarded in females with more emphasis than given to males. As they age, girls often respond to the socialization experiences with behavior that is rewarded and emphasized to the extent it becomes a major part of her self. Through gendered socialization practices, the internalization of ideas of what is a mother are communicated in many different forms and in a wide range of contexts beginning at a very early age (such as children-oriented media) and persisting over the life span (such as in experiences in school and on the job) (Ogle et al., 1996). Consequently, the pervasiveness of this internalized, cultural message leads to a tendency for women to incorporate this view as a major part of their self-concept. However, a mother may not hold the mothering identity as important or it may become a very large part of who she is. But regardless of the extent to which a mother internalizes the identity, society assumes and expects that all mothers will embrace the identity and comply with the normative expectations of the role to the fullest extent and judge her as if this is the case. The judgment of the identity also assumes all mothers have sufficient resources, homogeneous socialization experiences, and are not in an abusive relationship.

Socialization content and experiences vary by culture. Families from cultural backgrounds other than the dominant culture must manage not only the stress of childrearing, but also the stresses of acculturating into the dominant society and facing the biases and institutionalized social structural barriers to success that work against minorities and immigrants. The existence of these stressors can be attributed to persons with social and political power creating negative stereotypes of members of minority ethnic groups. Being a target of these stereotypes may influence one's beliefs and the socialization process that minority parents used with their children (Jambunathan, Burts, & Pierce, 2000, p. 395). Parenting patterns also vary for the poverty and lower-classes, that too must face institutional biases that make achieving all social expectations, including parenting, difficult. McLoyd's (1990) research indicates that lower education levels and increased amounts of stress among ethnic parents influences parent–child relations and practices. Parenting practices that fit those of European American mothers have higher levels of being deemed "appropriate" (Jambunathan et al., 2000) while deviations from the middle-class, white-parenting standards are viewed as bad mothering. Regardless, girls are socialized into the beliefs and practices of their culture and the result becomes a significant part of their identity as a mother.

The process of internalization is identity formation. For girls, the motherhood expectations of their culture receive more emphasis than most other female roles and the identity of mother becomes a master status. It so core to a female who is a mother that it becomes her label and self-reference. When attempting to fulfill her mother identity, she is attempting to fulfill a set of structures or norms that are expected of a person holding this identity. Additionally, girls are taught that the judgments of others are more important than her judgment of herself (Lerner, 1980). This places the judgments of others as the supreme reference for self-concept. Other-evaluation of identity fulfillment is important and affects action.

Identities are powerful forces of action. Stryker (1968) defined the self as a set of internalized roles and links role behavior and commitment to the salience of identities. In addition to identity norms, socialization creates a rank ordering based on the saliency of identities that results in some internalized roles being more important than others. To meet the expectations of the salient identities, role behavior occurs as actors seek opportunities to engage in that role. Consequently, the identity becomes the crux of self-perception which, in turn, again affects behavior due to a motivation to fulfill expectations compatible with self-structure (Markus, 1977). Individuals strive to "live up to their role" and enact a role in accordance with expectations associated with it. This makes the environment in which they enact the role very important. A mother can maintain her self-identification as a "good" mother only in an environment that confirms the good mother identity and allows her opportunities to meet the expectations. Disruption of this context or being unable to maintain such an environment threatens the mother's subjective reality. A breakdown in this environment then becomes a threat to an important identity and the mother's overall perception of self.

Similarly, McCall and Simmon's (1966) *role identity model* views an individual's identities as a loosely organized hierarchy of salience. The salience of an identity reflects the extent to which the image of self associated with it (i.e., role identity) corresponds to the individual's broader, abstract ideals, or in this case, the mothering ideology. The saliency of the identity leads to emotional responses based on the self-reflected conclusion of whether the mother is a "good" or "bad" mother. Her conclusion is rooted in abstract, external expectations that women, in the course of socialization, internalize as "mother." Once internalized and core to her identity, the role of mother becomes objectified and self-reflected. This part of the person is the "social self" which is "experienced as distinct and ever confronting the self in its totality" (Berger, 1966, p. 73). In other words, once the mother identity becomes a part of her that can be observed as a set of expectations (and hence failure), she can observe that part as separate from herself and her action and draw conclusions about how well she fills the identity. At the point of self-observation, the mother identity is prominent and is "the extent to which identities are associated with a strength of feeling" (Nuttbrock & Freudiger, 1991, p. 147).

LaRossa (1986) addresses the how the judgment of others become self-judgment and describes the hierarchy of the parental role as a social institution in which "certain goals, values, beliefs, and norms are associated with having children [...] people who become parents are perceived and treated differently based on the expectations individuals and society hold for parents" (p. 10). More importantly, mothers *internalize* the expectations and, due to identity saliency, come to evaluate their ability to care for and control their children based on their *own* perceptions of how others judge them regarding fulfillment of the obligations expected of the social identity. This is the judgment from society that mothers cannot escape – the presence of the expectations of the social institutions are ever-present in her mind and as a socially objectified reality, have immense power over her.

The strain of mothering is intensified by the power of the socially institutionalized expectations. Social institutions have power over a mother by imposing rigid, moral obligations that are core to her social identity. The obligations are not spontaneous but have a long history (Berger & Luckmann, 1966) that imposes social imperatives that maintain the mothering ideology and sustain social class power differences and male dominance. The history of the social institution of parenting that creates its power and totality over the expectations and identity of the mother is tantamount to law, both formal and informal. The ability to meet the expectations is contingent on the clarity of these formalized rules or laws that are often defined through the media. However, given the rapid intensification of mothering (Hays, 1996) occurring during the stalled revolution (Hochschild, 1989), the knowledge is anomic and unavailable on a practical level.

This history has power over the mother through the preexisting norms expected of her childcare role taking. Perceiving herself as not fulfilling the role increases her role strain and, as this strain becomes greater, her tendency will be to merge the role with herself even more. The unresolved problems are difficult to set aside and her investment in fulfilling the role can become unrelenting, especially in times of crisis.

> The amount of strain produced by low role adequacy is directly related to the extent of identification with that role, and [...] undergoing and coping with strain in a role is a way of investing

in the role, making it more difficult, rather than easier, to shed it.
(Turner, 1978, p. 16)

Another way the social institution of parenting sustains its power is by limiting the range of alternative behaviors. This ensures stability and maintenance of the motherhood norms. To allow mothers to do otherwise, threatens the social institution of mothering and the family with change. The limitations are a form of power that gains compliance with oppressive structures of inequality and serve as a social control function — a capability of the strongest to make their values count by crushing others (Giddens, 1979). Beyond the power of judgment by others, the power of the criminal justice system and social services over mothering are prime examples of the powerlessness mothers have in the state of affairs defined by the mothering ideology. As summed by Merton (1938):

> It is only when a system of cultural values extols, virtually above all else, certain common symbols of success for the population at large while its social structure rigorously restricts or completely eliminates access to approved modes of acquiring these symbols for a considerable part of the same population, that antisocial behavior ensues on a considerable scale. (p. 677)

The symbols of good mothering are universally extolled but the symbols of bad mothering may be extolled even more so. A crying baby is a significant symbol for the population at large and means the mother is struggling or failing to make her baby happy. The emphasis is on maternal responsibility while taking for granted a cultural model of natural, intensive, self-sacrificing, and isolated motherhood. The focus for the source of the problem is on the mother's behavior, not society, or unrealistic norms (Hays, 1996; Wall, 2001). Arguably, all mothers can improve their interactions with their children but when the focus of change is solely on the mother and rarely on the society, needed change to the mothering ideology will not be recognized. And the criminal justice system and social services enforce this focus by enforcing the expectations of "good" mothering.

3.5. Enforcing the Ideology: The Criminalization of "Poor" Mothering

The social institution of government has regulatory power over the mother by the preexisting norms and laws that define the expectations of a mother in her child caring role. These norms are enforced external to her self-judgments, are an object outside of her, and have power over her. As formal societal response, social services, and the criminal justice system claim authority over mothers by imposing sanctions that maintain institutional order and reproduce the motherhood ideology. A criminal justice response that upholds "good" mothering necessarily upholds the social institution. This makes the court system complicit in the cultural inequality inherent in the mothering ideology and legitimates it by rigidly enforcing the unrealistic expectations. Mothers who deviate from the ideals of motherhood are constructed as bad mothers, thereby justifying their social and legal regulation. For example, as found by Kline's (1995) research on the ideology of motherhood and its enforcement in the courts toward Native American mothers, the mothers were constructed in the court proceedings as "not meeting the dominant cultural and middle-class expectations that constitute the ideology of motherhood" (p. 119). Moreover, the courts viewed the mothers' intimate partner victimization as their own personal problem over which they should have control – "courts tend to characterize intimate partner violence as a personal problem or a problem of lifestyle and mothers who 'choose' to continue this lifestyle are being selfish" (p. 125). While this example focuses on minority mothers who are arguably even more vulnerable to biased criminal justice and social service practices than white mothers, all mothers who fail to meet the expectations can be treated criminally to some degree. Parenting practices of the poor and marginalized are subject to heightened scrutiny (Gurevich, 2008; Kline, 1995) and have a greater likelihood of coming under the supervision of child or family protective services, other social service agencies, and the civil or criminal courts.

Regardless of the unreality of the middle-class standards, social structures dominate the expectations and actions under which mothers operate and condition their "choice" to follow the norms. To allow a mother to choose to parent otherwise suggests that a mother has agency and power over the social institution of parenting (Giddens, 1979). And while this domination is claimed to be a necessary feature of social institutions, the social services and criminal justice response to mothers makes having the choice to act other than what is expected a false choice. She is powerless to change the expectations and therefore cannot escape the social demands of mothering. If she does not follow the mothering norms, society imposes negative consequences and strips her of a core identity of women – "good mother." This identity loss and fear of negative repercussions from social services and the criminal justice system do not move her toward rational action toward her child, but rather the identity loss moves her toward heightened emotion and the loss of rationalization (to be discussed in the next chapter). Additionally, mothers do not have the economic relief to meet the middle-class standards imposed by these systems. And, given the stalled revolution, even middle-class mothers cannot find the time or money required for "good" mothering. Gurevich's (2008) work on mothering finds that "today's 'good' mother is a 'total' mother whose existence is defined in terms of her child's real and perceived needs – a modern, expert-defined, and culturally middle-class (and white) creation" (p. 521). A child's *real* needs are shelter, food, emotional and cognitive development, and healthcare. The *perceived* needs are those interpreted by the mother and are not always readily apparent. Especially since infants do not have verbal skills to communicate their needs. Consequently, the perception of what the needs are is heavily influenced by the mothering ideology as mothers strive to determine a response that will immediately assuage a crying baby.

Mothers who request social support are "bad" mothers, especially if her family form is not the traditional, two-parent, white middle-class family. However, as Gurevich finds "if she is a single parent without means and social support, [then as] a 'good' mother [she] must admit to and practice dependency on the state and medical establishment" (2008, p. 521). In other words, women who reject such dependency on social services are "bad" women. This irony underscores the cultural contradiction of what is thought and what is rewarded. Mothers who cannot meet the middle-class standard must present themselves as "bad" mothers and endure the stigma and subsequent negative consequences to gain state support. This presentation of self is required in order to comply with criminal justice and social service judgments.

Criminal justice and social service practices, especially civil and criminal trials, are highly visible actions that sustain the mothering ideology through boundary maintenance. These status-degradation ceremonies (Garfinkel, 1965) formalize her inadequacy by mandating supervision over her and by criminalizing "bad" behavior. This has a norm-delineating or boundary maintenance function (Durkheim, 1895; Gurevich, 2008) with the legal proceedings creating "normalization" (Foucault, 1979) of the expectations of the mothering ideology. The trial stigmatizes and punishes women for being "bad mothers" and makes public examples of mothers who fall outside the courts' perception of "good" mothering. However, the court's perception is founded also in the anomic, unrealistic mothering ideology and creates a self-fulfilling prophecy of "bad" mothers and stereotypes of mothers in socially marginalized groups, especially women of color.

Unfortunately, this is true also for the social service component of society due to the perception of clients. Social workers are not perceived as "helpers" or "helpful" among the poor. And among the other classes, these perceptions are perceived as a threat of judgment or negative evaluation. Even if the social work is well intended, supportive, and positive, there is worry on the part of the recipient about what society at large will think. Consequently, social service workers face two challenges. One is the perception of the client that the workers will judge and evaluate them − that the workers represent society. The second is that the workers must abide by legal requirements and liabilities. Workers do not have control over legal issues or supervisors who will impose requirements on them. The ability to be a buffer between the client and the law is very slippery and soon the worker will find that he/she does not have the decision-making power or authority to manage the case according to their own judgments. The case is then out of the worker's hands and the client regrets calling for help because the worker cannot promise that the law will not get involved or that a certain path of assistance will occur. For these reasons, mothers in need of social support often do not seek it or continue receiving it. The workers may willingly enforce the "good" mother boundaries by initiating proceedings or revoking support or they may be compelled by law to take such action. Either way, willingly or unwillingly, they are enforcers of the institutionalized, legally mandated perceptions of good mothering based on middle-class standards.

Discourse is a major force in defining and stigmatizing mothers. For the court system and social services, the professionalization of medical, psychiatric, and administrative personnel transmits the standards by which a mother is judged "fit" and a mother who "acts otherwise" to the institutionalized expectations is medicalized as a dysfunctional person. This is demonstrated by "the acceptance of the EED (Extreme Emotional Disorder) legal defense and the attendant power of the medical establishment to construct and define the norms of maternal behavior and demeanor" (Gurevich, 2008, p. 525). Defense attorneys are major players in the professional discourse because "the struggle of attorneys to find the best accounts for their clients turns courtroom transcripts into excellent barometers of what is said and thought in a culture at any given moment of time" (Ferguson, 1996, p. 87).

Historically, this has not been the case. At the beginning of the twentieth century, all public and criminal justice scrutiny focused on the conditions and suffering of the mother, especially abandonment by her husband, and the infant victim was not discussed. A mental institution was considered much more appropriate than a prison. The mother was often portrayed as a victim of poverty, shame, and distress (Grey, 2015). By the end of that century, the focus was on the victim and the mother is viewed with no sympathy and the typical response is prison or, more recently, the death penalty. The intensification of the mothering ideology has resulted in a harsher criminal justice response and greater surveillance by social services.

In the end, there is no escaping the negative label that goes with seeking assistance. Informal assistance from family and friends carries a negative label also but perhaps that label is more pliable and temporary than those given by the criminal justice system and social services. A capitalist society views a person who needs help as weak or lazy.

State regulation of mothers receiving assistance would not be an issue or as necessary as it is now if mothering were realistic, less anomic, and social and culturally supported. Removal of inequity and the addition of nonstigmatizing, legally separate social support would greatly reduce the need for "regulating" mothering. Now, with the criminalization of bad mothering, the consequence of the power of the institutionalized motherhood ideology and its enforcement through social and legal channels is that mothers find themselves in a situated context fraught with suffering. Not only must they raise a child while managing confusing and contradictory expectations of mothering, they must do so in a demoralized state.

3.6.   The Situated Context and Demoralization

All mothers ultimately share a recognition of the ideology of intensive mothering and that if you are a "good" mother, you must be an intensive one (Hays, 1996). At the same time, all mothers live in a society where child rearing is generally devalued and the primary emphasis is placed on profit, efficiency, and "getting ahead." This is a cultural contradiction where the goals of the family social institution conflict with the economic and government social institutions (Hays, 1996). Due to this mismatch and the anomic state of parenting, mothers do not completely know nor can they fully articulate the universal ideology or expectations of mothering. Mothering in this context requires persevering through action without certainty that her actions will fulfill the expectation or manage the crying baby. "To know how to go on is not necessarily, or normally, to be able to formulate clearly what the rules are [...] The [mother] *must* first "know" in order to know right from wrong" (Giddens, 1979, pp. 67–93). In other words, without a clear knowledge of what to do, a person does not know right from wrong and it is unclear what the correct course of action should be, which is the essence of anomia. But in the face of the failing symbol of a crying baby, she is compelled to act. This creates variations on the content of "correct" mothering on her part as well as tension from having to choose between conflicting goals and ideas of how to parent that can result in even more confusing and unclear expectations. This is characteristic of secondary socialization into a specialized role that is fraught with anomic content. Berger and Luckmann (1967) point to the abstractness of secondary socialization and claims it "makes the subjective reality of its internalizations even more vulnerable to challenging definitions of reality, [...] [because] socialization is never complete and the contents face continuing threats" (p. 148). Within an ideology, there is space for confusion and uncertainty. The greater the amount of challenge and hence confusion, the less there is a clear sense of priority among the content or whether the requirements are being met.

Despite the lack of clarity and completeness of socialization into the mother role, mothers can articulate the expectations and behaviors of a "good" mother in broad, vague terms. What they cannot easily do is apply or adapt these general rules to immediate situations, especially when they are operating under stressful conditions such as no resources, sick children, lack of sleep (Stanton et al., 2000), abuse, and inconsolable children. Without being able to articulate the expectations that constrain and strain them, they must do constant intellectual and emotion work on how to "go on" or typically act. Under these circumstances, mothers must "attempt to resolve their feelings of inadequacy by returning to [...] the ideology of intensive mothering" (Hays, 1996, p. 134). In this way, the unclear expectations become circular and lack even more clarity. Often these attempts fail because the ideology is vague and contradictory. But regardless of the conflicting, unclear interpretations of the expectations, it is the outcome (such as a well, happy baby or gaining needed resources) that tells them whether they have successfully met the expectations. Being able to achieve the desired outcome is having agency even if achieved in a haphazard way. Power to affect a desired end is the agency mothers seek to demonstrate and an ability to describe the rules is less important (Giddens, 1979).

The capitalistic, child-rearing industry may be doing more harm than good in clarifying effective mothering behavior. Aside from sustaining and creating expectations of mothering, the child-rearing industry pushes methods for achieving them – permissive versus progressive parenting; negotiation versus "rules are rules"; traditional versus modern; and child-centered versus adult-centered, to name a few. The constant barrage of new material generated by this industry for the purpose of making money constantly increases the already unrealistically long list of "expert" advice on what mothers should achieve and how they should achieve it. Consider the numerous books, magazines, and child-rearing courses that are sold everyday. In order for a new book, magazine article, or course to be published and advertised, it must give new advice on goals, methods, and behaviors of parenting. This results in a continually growing list with no end in sight. Moreover, the new expectations and methods largely go untested scientifically. There is little scientific support that many of these expert ideas produce the outcome promised.

Regardless of which method of caregiving a mother attempts to use to manage a crying child and how many different methods are produced by the child-rearing industry, there are fundamental, universal goals, or outcomes of mothering. What a mother can and must do is assuage a crying baby, keep the baby healthy, and train the baby to eat, sleep, and use a toilet. Failing to do these basic outcomes is universally viewed as failing to be a good mother. These socially expected outcomes are at a more basic level than belief in methodology (Baca Zinn, 1990; Dill, 1994; Taylor, 2011) and it is clear when they are not fulfilled. It is not clear when a proscribed method has worked better than other methods or maternal actions. Primacy in the belief of the methods with little systematic focus on whether they produce the desired outcome makes the mothering ideology more confusing. Indeed, the nonuniversality of the belief in method, rather than the more universal outcomes of mothering, contributes to the strainful, demoralizing environment of maternal suffering.

The basic outcomes, the core mother identity, and the power of the mothering ideology are central to my argument. A baby's actions are the significant symbols of these universals. Hence, the phrase "a crying baby" captures the concrete attempts at good mothering that are not succeeding at upholding the identity and fulfilling the ideology. Crying is a significant symbol to everyone that something is not working and an adjustment needs to be made. And, as myself (Smithey, 1997, 1998), and many others find (e.g., Gottesman, 2007), mothers view infant crying as a negative reflection on their ability to parent, thereby increasing their distress. The haphazard attempts at "good" mothering can produce a volatile home setting. And, given the typical isolation of the mother—infant context, often there is no third party who can assist with caring for the child or intervene in the case of violence. The crying child is symbolic of the failure that is caused by the social context of mothering under difficult conditions, including unrealistic, anomic expectations of intensive mothering, lack of economic resources, unsupportive or abusive intimate partnerships, reduced privacy and freedom, social isolation, a challenged identity, and the inability to escape the stressful, emotionally escalating context.

The failed attempts to meet the expectations heighten the emotions of the mothers and reduce rationality. A person can return to a failing ideology only so many times before she stops the attempts to intelligently reflect on her actions. These stops leave the situation prone to violence. This context and the repetitive cycle of failing attempts leave many mothers feeling overwhelmed with the caretaking role (Mugavin, 2005). Ogle et al. (1996) liken predisposing chronic stress to living in an urban location (p. 182). There is an increased physiological arousal because of the physical difficulties of dealing with the environment and the chronic assault on the senses caused by crowding, noise, pollution, and the loss of personal space and quiet time for rest and recuperation from the rigors of daily life. Post-partum environments entail the same chronic assault. This analogy applies to the social construction of unrealistic expectations of parenting and the inability to escape that chronically assault the senses and which ultimately create the cascade of negative affect breaking down the coping mechanism of constant reinterpretation of anger-provoking interaction into guilt. Once the breakdown of coping mechanisms occurs, the result is an escalation of violence and heightened emotion (cascade of anger) that catapults the cultural message of good mothering out the door.

A demoralized state has also been found to be a factor in female-perpetrated homicide of adult victims (Jensen, 2001). Women resort to homicide as a result of suffering situational stresses that act as triggers. The chronicity of the suffering requires coping mechanisms and anger management skills that eventually become insufficient to survive the fatigue and lack of tangible, immediate reward of intensive care of another person. For women with "damaged selves" (Crimmins et al., 1997), the coping mechanisms are even more fragile. Damaged persons do not have sufficient experience with intimate interactions that result in a positive self-evaluation to do the required emotional work.

Under these chronic, demoralizing conditions, all it takes is a crying baby for a breakdown in reality to occur.

Chapter 4

A Crying Baby: The Situated Context of Infanticide

She would cry a lot, and I had to take her to the hospital a lot, they said nothing was wrong with her, I gave her a lot to eat and stuff, I didn't know what was wrong with her, she would just cry and cry and cry and wouldn't stop. I tried everything — talking, walking, rocking. I sang to her. Nothing worked. [Did you sleep much at night?] No.

Infanticidal mothers describe a history of struggle and suffering as they tried to meet the gendered expectations of the mothering ideology: assuage a crying baby, make a sick baby well, do the emotion work necessary to meet the demands of the baby, take care of a baby with insufficient economic resources or emotional support, and, in some cases, appease social services and the court system.

In this chapter, I frame the context of the occurrence of infanticide within a symbolic interactionism perspective using Luckenbill's (1977) stages of homicide as a situated transaction (see Table 4.1). Into this theoretical frame, I integrate Mead's (1934) game and role-taking, Goffman's (1959,1967) saving face and presentation of self, Berger and Luckmann's (1966) social constructionism, and Giddens (1979, 1984) structured action. I make a sociological argument, the first part of which is found in this chapter, and explain how the increasingly anomic, unrealistic expectations of mothering create a context that can escalate into irrationality and violence.

Using Luckenbill's (1977) stages, I detail the process by which a mother comes to interpret her infant's crying negatively and becomes a challenge to her identity as a mother — a core, gender-socialized identity. As previously discussed, predispositional to this challenge are cultural inequality inherent in the gendered, often-contradictory beliefs of mothering and economic inequality of women. These predispositions are further exacerbated by the degree to which the baby is wanted. I explain how a context of cultural and economic inequality, strain, and anomic expectations of mothering require a mother to reflexively monitor and reflectively evaluate her actions, persevere, and do the accompanying emotion work to mask the struggle. In the cases of infanticide presented here, these requirements heightened emotion that lead to a fatal injury. I argue that the mother's persistence in negatively interpreting the infant's actions is the pivotal point where she begins to "lose it" and assaults her child. It is at this stage that the mother no longer steps back and reflects on her actions. She loses rationality as the emotions escalate and implements the most accessible power available to her — power over the baby.

Table 4.1. Luckenbill's Stages of Homicide as a Situated Transaction Applied to Infanticidea.

Stage I	Stage II	Stage III	Stage IV	Stage V
Initial action by victim	Interpretation by offender as noncompliance	Offender becomes more forceful in an attempt to restore order	Continued noncompliance by victim/ working agreement of violence is forged	Fatal injury by offender

Application to Infanticide:

Incessant crying; prolonged illness; difficult to train	Challenge to mother's identity as a "Good" mother, authority, or overall character	Typically shaking, yelling, hitting, or temporarily withdrawing	Escalation of activity and heightened emotion; forging of violence is by mother	Typically head trauma followed by abdomen trauma or overall battering of baby

Notes: Stage VI is not applied.

The application of a theoretical model requires establishing exogenous and endogenous boundaries. A transaction requires an identifiable starting point. My research data, research by other social scientists, and news media accounts most often show that parent-perpetrated infanticide starts with *a crying baby*. Although the mother–infant transactional pattern is replete with possible "starting" points, such as irregular sleep patterns, etc., I use crying by the baby as the identifiable starting point of the mother–infant transaction that challenges the mother because it significantly symbolizes the struggle of the mother. Analyzing my data sources and relevant data from other research on mothering (Adinkrah, 2001; Alder & Baker, 1997; Arnot, 1994; Barr, 1990; Briggs & Mantini-Briggs, 2000; Crittenden & Craig, 1990; d'Orban, 1979; Friedman et al., 2005; Goetting, 1988; Jackson, 2002; Mugavin, 2005; Oberman, 2003; Oberman & Meyer, 2001, 2008; Rose, 1986; Scott, 1973; Stroud, 2008), I situate the causes, frequency, and duration of the crying in a model of intense mother–infant interaction. The crying is often due to unclear causes and conflict as the mother attempts to train her infant to eat, sleep, and potty-train, or manage illness. I situate the details of the fatal assault in the economic and cultural inequalities of the mother to show how they create abnormal circumstances under which almost anyone would experience a higher proclivity toward violence. As found by Shaw and McKay's (1969) work on the ecology of crime, "normal people put in abnormal circumstances" are likely to use actions they would not otherwise use or believe they are capable of using (see also Bernard, 1990). In other words, these social conditions relentless battered and predisposed mothers toward violence.

4.1. A Crying Baby: Interpreting the Infant's Actions

4.1.1. Stage I: Initial Action by the Baby

Goffman (1967) defined a "situated transaction" as a chain of interaction between two or more individuals that lasts the time they find themselves in one another's immediate physical presence. The interaction mutually affects the interpretations and behavior of the actors. According to Hentig (1948), this applies to crime also where "the victim of a violent crime often shapes and moulds the criminal" (p. 384). This was later restated by Wolfgang (1958) who described criminal homicide as a collective transaction, "in many crimes, especially in criminal homicide, the victim is often a major contributor to the criminal act [...] the victim may be one of the major precipitating causes of his own demise" (p. 1).

Linking these premises, Luckenbill (1977) describes criminal homicide as "the culmination of an intense interchange between an offender and victim" (p. 177).

In the situated transaction of a mother-perpetrated infant homicide, the initial action of the victim is difficult to definitively state due to a history that can be traced back to conception. In the worst scenario, some babies are conceived in undesirable circumstances such as premarital or extramarital sex, teenage pregnancy, or in some cases, sexual assault. In these cases, some women choose to keep the baby due to personal beliefs and the baby's birth per se challenges the mother's identity as she reluctantly assumes the mothering role. Other women in these circumstances have abortions or carry the baby to term while concealing the pregnancy. In some cases of concealment, mothers commit neonaticide — the disposal of a newborn — usually by means of abandonment. The best-case scenario is a planned pregnancy that results in a loved and wanted baby. Even then, the circumstances of the conception can be the start of the challenge, whether negative or positive. Either way, for those who choose to raise the baby, the vast majority does so in the context of cultural and economic inequality and must manage challenging interactions with the infant, regardless of how wanted the child.

A crying baby is almost universally viewed as unpleasant (Green, Gustafson, Irwin, & Kalinowski, 1995). However, a crying baby does not have an emotionally, compelling impact on a mother *unless it is her own baby*. For mothers, crying has a dimension beyond just the unpleasant, ambient noise. When it is the mother's own baby, the crying is framed in a sense of responsibility that makes the mother feel that she must stop the crying. This feeling is based on the cultural mothering ideology that makes the mother responsible for stopping the crying thereby allowing her and others to judge whether she is a "good" mother. This judgment and the context of inequality are important for delineating the factors that underlie a mother's response to crying.

But all babies cry and many mothers experience the same struggle and suffering yet do not lethally injure their infants (Gottesman, 2007). So where is the line that, when crossed, results in serious assault and lethal injury? Is it accidental? Are the nonlethal events simply due to luck? Is there a clear threshold that most mothers never have to cross? To answer these questions, I deconstruct the fatal interaction of mothers and use crying or difficult care as the "initial" behavior by the victim for the starting point of the transaction. In my data and the data from other studies cited aforementioned, these mothers who have lethally injured their child stated crying as the primary reason. In these cases, the crying required the mother to act, her actions were unsuccessful, and she lethally assaulted her child.

According to Luckenbill's first stage, the opening move in the fatal transaction is an action by the victim that is subsequently defined by the mother as a challenge to her mother identity or an offense to "face," that is the image of self a person claims during a particular occasion or social context (Goffman, 1967). Phrases like "I didn't know what do" or "I didn't know what was wrong" show that the crying is a substantial stressor for the mother. The victim's activity, however, is a pivotal event that separates the previous occasioned activity of the offender and victim from their subsequent violent confrontation. There is a line that is crossed where the mother is not just, once again, attending to her crying baby. It is a line that, once crossed, is very difficult to cross back over. It represents a culmination of all her stressors; it is her "tipping point" toward heightened emotion. The mothers frequently describe incessant crying, prolonged illness, and difficulty in training (e.g., feeding, sleep schedules, and toilet training) as the initial stressors in crossing the line into an intense, fatal interchange. The following data demonstrate the challenge posed by a baby crying with no clear cause. For example:

> [...] he was always crying and always needing my attention. I tried feeding him all the time, he just wouldn't eat right. I didn't know what to do.

> He was very difficult to take care of and was taking up an awful amount of my time. His crying was driving me crazy.

> I didn't know what to do. He would just cry. He wouldn't stop.

> The crying and constant need for attention made me lose control. I held it in as long as I could.

In other cases, attempts at training the baby resulted in prolonged crying. For example,

> When I went back into the living room, the baby was asleep. I woke her up because she had on some the clothes I was going

to wash. When I picked her up she had peed on herself. So I took her into the bathroom and I closed the door. I took her to the toilet bowl and pointed at it. I said "why didn't you say peepee?" and she just said no and started crying. The more I tried to get her to go to the bathroom, the louder and harder she cried.

Atypically ill infants increase the demand for care and emotion work and have been found to contribute to nonlethal assaults of children (Straus & Gelles, 1990; Wade, Black, & Ward-Smith, 2005). Studying mothers of colicky infants, Levitzky and Cooper (2001) find that 70% of mothers of colicky infants had explicit aggressive thoughts toward their infants and 26% of these mothers had infanticidal thoughts during the infant's episodes of colic. Gottesman (2007) reports that colic occurs in up to 28% of infants across all categories of gender, race, and social class. Studies by Green et al. (1995) on crying acoustics, find the sounds of crying and the perception attributed to the acoustics are different for normal infants compared with infants who are sick. Data from my interviews corroborate these findings.

Uh, he was mainly sick all the time, he stayed sick, basically it was an everyday thing trying to make it.

[...] he had asthma, uh, he stayed real cold all the time, started throwing up a few days before he died.

In one case, the mother was dealing with the tedious, daily care of an encephalitic baby.

He was born with, uh, hydro, um, encephalitis. He had four surgeries, and a shunt that ran from his head into his stomach to drain fluid. He had sleep apnea due to a heart murmur (the baby was also taking Deophalin, a medication used to develop the lungs). I had a sick baby everyday. I didn't think I would make it.

Mugavin (2005) also reports a case of an encephalitic infant that was fatally injured due to frustration and the increased demand for care.

In these cases, the mother's struggle to meet the expectation of a noncrying baby, potty-training, and care for a chronically ill child is evident. The compulsion to achieve this goal leads to negative self-perception and the mother is challenged to meet the goal.

4.1.2. Stage II: The Mother Interprets the Baby's Previous Move as Personally Offensive

The combination of the common traits of a mother being "primarily responsible for the child" and "persistent crying" by the child, lead to the perception of "the child's behavior as disobedient, defiant, or emotionally unresponsive" (Friedman et al., 2005, p. 1581). This seeming lack of control over the baby interacts with the incessant crying and difficulty in training and threatens the mother's perception of herself as a capable parent, her self-esteem, authority, or overall character. As discussed in the previous chapter, the mothering ideology consists of institutionalized goals, values, beliefs, and expectations that are required for "good" mothering. Mothering is perceived differently from other roles, including fathering, and is judged accordingly by everyone. Based on the mothering ideology, mothers in these cases negatively self-evaluate their own ability to care for and control their children. Gottesman (2007), studying infant crying, finds also that "parents may also view infant crying as a negative reflection on their ability to parent, increasing their distress" (p. 333).

The following data describe some of the normative expectations the mothers had for themselves as well as for their infant. The self-judgment and sense of helplessness are evident in phrases such as "I thought I could do it, but I couldn't," "I could not," "It's my fault," and "I guess (my mom) is a better mother."

> She would cry and cry. Then I would start crying. I didn't know how to make her stop. I thought I could do it (raise a child), but I couldn't.

> I now realize there was a lot more to it (raising a child) than I thought. I wanted to do a good job but I couldn't get him (the infant) to do the right things. [What do you mean by right things?] You know, sleep all night, eat at certain times of the day, that kind of thing.

> He was a very fussy baby and I could not soothe him. It's my fault. I could not help him.

> My first child was a very good baby causing no problems. My second was very fussy, I could not calm him down and, no matter what, I could not do it.

The held, unrealistic expectations play a role in setting the mother up for failure. The gender socialized "fairy tale" ideas of raising children did not prepare her for the reality of raising children.

> [Before the baby was born, what did you think being a good mom meant?] A good mom is always having food in the house, thinking about a roof over the head and being there when the kids were home. I'd be getting them things, like you never had, you know, just being there mostly. [Did you think about the crying, staying up late, feeding?] Well, at first it was probably by

oldest son, you know, I didn't think it would be that hard. But then my mom mostly raised my oldest son. I guess 'cause I was so young, you know, and she was like, [...] she spoiled him, she made it much more easier. I guess she's a better mother.

I always wanted a little girl. [What did you think having a little girl would be like?] It would be fun, you know I would comb her hair and dress her in those pretty dresses and stuff. I always wanted a little girl, when I was a child I always played with dolls and stuff. It didn't turn out that way. She wouldn't do it.

When I was pregnant, I was happy. I knew I would be able to do things as mother–daughter do — share, talk, to be open. I did not have these things with my mother.

In one case, the mother's expectations of raising a baby were contingent on gender.

I always wanted a boy, you have to protect girls more, take care of them more.

In other cases, significant others enforced the "good" mother expectation of assuaging a crying baby. In the following cases, the father's expectations of the baby and his expectations of the mother to stop the crying baby resulted in stress and negative self-feelings for the mother.

He wanted the baby to have everything we didn't have when we grew up — like not having a father at home. It was like a fairy tale, he had images of picnics, not having to be separated, the baby not having stepparents, he never wanted us to separate. Everything was shattered when the baby was born. He (the husband) was always yelling at me to get the baby, to make the baby stop crying. We started fighting all the time; he blamed me when the baby cried.

I tried to keep him from disturbing my husband, so when he (the infant) cried I would jump up and get him as quickly as I could and stayed up all night trying to keep him quiet.

In all these cases, the subject viewed the unmet expectations as a threat to her ability to parent that, in turn, threatened her self-esteem. This is congruent with Kaplan's work (1986) on self-referent behavior that explains negative self-attitude as a consequence of derogating experiences. Self-referent behavior is looked upon as a mediating link between the self-referring person and the social structure within which the person participates. There is a need to accept oneself as approximating a general standard present in the social structure of the current situation. The behaviors that do not fit become salient and remain so until the self-evaluation is satisfied.

The saliency is because social contexts that invoke the mothering ideology require mothers to find a way to successfully meet the expectations of the ideology. To achieve this, mothers must anticipate and interpret the infant's actions. This is particularly problematic because infants do not have cognitive or communicative capacity to assist in the interpretation. Instead, she is left guessing. In some cases, the guessing is incorrect and her attempts at "good" mothering repeatedly fail, either in an immediate series of attempts or periodically over a short period of time. As this point, some mothers use force.

4.1.3.   Stage III: The Mother Becomes More Forceful in an Attempt to Restore Order

Unrealistic and unmet expectations of mothers have been associated with violence toward children (Azar, Stevenson, & Johnson, 2012; McGreier & Azar, 2016). Unable to gain compliance with the expectations from the baby, the mother attempts to restore the order (meaning making her baby happy and well) and reaffirm face (Goffman, 1967) by "standing her ground." She is compelled by her belief in the mothering ideology to achieve the expected outcome of a noncrying baby. Her choice becomes repeating the same action or increasing her use of force in an attempt to gain compliance. Choosing force, she repeats the actions she believes would stop the crying or result in wellness or successful training, only with more intensity. This escalates into a power struggle in an effort to "win" the contest. Unfortunately, at this point in the transaction there is only one type of power that is easily available to her — power over the baby.

There are three types of power relevant to being a mother. The first is *power over the baby* that can become increasingly forceful when she is unable to successfully mother. But the power is one-sided and only exists over the baby. The baby does not have the power to respond or protect itself. The use of power through increasing force is the easiest to implement and becomes apparent in the following data.

> We (the mother and her boyfriend) was (sic) having trouble potty training him. We made him sit on the potty for an hour. Then (the boyfriend) beat him. I made him sit on the potty some more, then I whupped him good.

Korbin's (1986) work finds that many battering mothers perceived their child as rejecting of her and malevolent. Azar et al. (2016) find that unrealistic expectations foster hostile attributions of children's intent. Totman (1978) reports also that the infanticidal mothers viewed their children as irritants and symbolic of their confinement, frustration, and failure. Motz (2001) described the infanticidal mothers in her research as turning their passive role of trapped mother into an active one in which she is in control, as the "aggressor." My interview data find the same and show an increase in force and an interpretation of defiance. Phrases like "she wouldn't eat," "he wouldn't listen," and "he didn't care" show how the mother, at this stage of the transaction continues interpreting the baby's actions as willful defiance.

> I couldn't get her to eat so I put her in her room for a while. She cried and I thought now maybe she'll eat. She kept crying and wouldn't eat. I put her on the floor and left the room. I could still hear her crying. I went back in the living room and hit her and told her she had to eat. She still wouldn't eat.

> (She had beaten the baby with a belt and buckle because she had been wetting her pants too often. Earlier her boyfriend had told her that the babysitter had complained that she had wet her clothes while at the babysitter's home.) I went into the bathroom and took a shower. When I got out of the shower, I got the dirty clothes ready so I could do the laundry. He had used it on himself again. He wouldn't listen.

> He was fine that morning, he had got up about six something and we went to take care of some stuff (run errands) and the baby had used it (urinated) on himself. Then, I made him sit in the corner. Later he used it again, then I whupped him. Nothing stopped him. Whuppings, sittin' in the corner, he didn't care.

The second type is *power over self* and consists of the mother's ability to stop her unsuccessful actions and step-back to assess her attempts at meeting the expectations. Attempts to have power over herself are demonstrated with phrases like "I put her on the floor and left the room." Power over self is due to socialization experiences, self-esteem, and reflexive monitoring and reflective intelligence. The ability to garner this power is effected by her predisposed state described in Chapter 2. Crimmins et al. (1997) offer a self-psychology perspective that suggests maternal infanticide results from mothers who have damaged selves. Focusing on the childhood experiences of offending mothers, they attribute the damaged self to a lack of maternal affection. They refer to this intergenerational transmission as a cycle of poor or "absent mothering" that would model appropriate maternal behavior. Those who are not subject to this modeling are said to have a "damaged self" of insufficient content for caring. Damaged mothers were not socialized into models that offer a range of options for the care and management of children. They have not experienced or have not witnessed successful mothering behaviors and their personal stock of knowledge is limited with very few options from which to draw. This reduces her power over herself.

The expectations of the mothering ideology appear to be very specific behaviors in the mothers' minds and not ranges of appropriate behavior. The power over self that is most effective for avoiding violence in this situation is the ability to find the range of socially acceptable behaviors that fall within the variation of the specific expectation. Falling outside the socially acceptable range of mothering behaviors is deviant, possibly criminal, and viewed by society as "bad" mothering. Confirming questions of face and self is correlated with the ability to step back and is self-fulfilling. The more a mother realizes she can step back and "practices" stepping back, the more this becomes incorporated into the rehearsals or attempts to assuage the crying baby. The stepping back behaviors become prominent in the self-perception and identity of "good mother" and as a person in control. Her ability to use this power is contingent on the amount of emotion work she has endured, how demoralized she is, her economic resources, her support mechanisms, her life experiences, and her self-esteem. Rehearsals do not always yield improvement in the mother–child interactions. The strain of finding a solution to a crying baby may constrain a mother's ability to be flexible and learn from the negative consequences of her behavior (Azur et al., 2016). Moreover, she loses the ability to recognize that she is becoming more forceful. Consequently, when the attempts at solutions are depleted, she is less likely to step back and more likely use violence due to its ease of access.

The third type of power is *power to change or not adhere to the socially institutionalized behaviors* and is the most difficult to exercise. For mothers, this power consists of consciously deciding to set aside her belief in the mothering ideology and redefine the expectations of good mothering in her own terms of success. For example, deciding to not attempt potty training until age four. Social institutions limit the range of alternative behaviors to her to ensure stability and maintenance of the norms. To allow mothers to do other than the socially institutionalize norms of "good" mothering, threatens the institution with change. It also threatens the oppressive structures of inequality and the ability to socially control women and, therefore, patriarchy. The mother is powerless to change the ideology because to have the power to change the internalized expectations and rehearsed activities that should restore order, is to have power over one's socialization and identity formation. It is also to have power over the institutionalized expectations. Using an alternative action would also confirm questions of face and self perceived by the offender as being raised by the victim (Goffman, 1967) with the mother demonstrating power over the institution. To change the expectations of the institution requires social movements and even then, the change is slow, often taking a generation or more.

All three forms of power are immediate forces in mother–infant interactions. She is caught in a duality between investing her energy in the easiest, most accessible form of power – power over the infant – and the most difficult form to access – power over the institutionalized expectations. Most often, mothers persevere and hang in the balance between the two powers and have many rehearsals of stepping back and rethinking her behavior and the current situation. This produces no real change in the circumstances but women are taught to put a "smile on their face" and continue persevering as if there is no conflict. In cases of violence, the balance is tipped toward the lowest level of power the mother has in the immediate context, which is over the socially institutionalized expectations of "good" mothering. It is this powerlessness to meet these expectations that moves her away from the rational power over herself, that is, "stepping-back," and moves her toward continued, negative interpretations of her infant's actions as noncompliant behavior challenging her identity. At this point, her greatest power, that is, her power over the infant, becomes violence as the baby's actions increasingly become viewed as willful noncompliance.

4.1.4. Stage IV: Continued Noncompliance by the Baby

As previously stated, mothers attempt to reduce the noncompliance with increasing force or make attempts to withdraw from the infant to avoid becoming more forceful. For example,

> I kept yellin' and yellin' and he just cried louder and louder. [...]
> So I shut myself in my room. I could still hear him crying, he just
> wouldn't shut up. The longer I was in my room the louder he
> cried. He finally came to my door and was crying at my door.

However, as illustrated earlier, the increased force or withdrawal did not reduce the infant's noncompliance but rather increased it. Yelling at, hitting, or even walking away from a crying baby results in louder cries as the baby attempts to make its mother aware of its discomfort. The escalation of activity and heightened emotion by both the mother and infant is accompanied by an increase in irrationality once the mother reaches higher levels of emotion. For example, the story at the beginning of Chapter 2 illustrates the mother's rage,

> The baby awaked from his nap and started crying. The baby was
> on the couch when I hit him. I hit him with the back of my hand
> on the side. I put him back on the couch and he started crying,
> then I shook him and starting hitting him.

In one case, the mother is asking an infant to shut up. This demonstrates a desperate, irrational tactic that expects an infant to not only understand the request, but to have the cognitive capacity to determine a behavior that complies with the request.

> I asked him and asked him to shut up, I finally shook him. He
> stopped crying, then I put him down and he started it up again.

In another case, the mother comes to believe the baby has the cognitive and behavioral capacity to make her continue to hold her baby.

> I tried everything, you know, I hit her and hit her, she wouldn't
> let me put her down.

The perceived willful noncompliance increases the mother's emotional stake and made her irrational. Studying abusive mothers, Korbin (1986) concludes that many battering mothers perceived their children as rejecting and many perceived their development as outside the normal range. Some perceived their children as malevolent. Stroud (2008) concludes the same, "the thinking, perceptions, and emotions shortly before the time of the [infanticide] were delusional," (p. 491). It is this state of high emotion, irrationality, and delusional that makes the battering so severe that the baby is fatally injured.

There are three categories of mothers who "lose it." One category is "battering moms" (Alder & Baker, 1997; Crimmins et al., 1997; d'Orban, 1979; Oberman & Meyer, 2001, 2008; Stroud, 2008) who have had many rehearsals using aggression to gain compliance from the infant. For these mothers, there have been prior episodes of "losing it" but without the infliction of a lethal injury. The second category is mothers who do not have a history of hitting the baby but "lose it" during the only episode of aggression and, unfortunately, inflict a lethal injury. "Losing it" intersects with the physiological vulnerability of the infant. For younger infants, the high level of physiological vulnerability increases the likelihood of any blow being lethal. In other words, a two year old has a much greater chance of surviving a blow to the head or abdomen than a two month old. The two-year-old simply has a stronger body. For infants, one blow to the head in one bad moment can be lethal (DiMaio & DiMaio, 2001).

The third category is a mother who frequently uses severe violence to control or "discipline" her child. These mothers are more likely to have some form of mental illness and have an abnormal need to hurt people and their children are the most accessible and over whom she has the most power. Also in this category are mothers who are caught in a cycle of violence of constant physical assault as a means of discipline due to belief in the need to beat bad behavior out of their children (Straus, 2001).

For any category, there is a challenge to the mother identity that is crucial for understanding not only how these mothers came to lethally injure their children, but to understand how any mother can be challenged and could, due to the power the mothering ideology has over her, find herself assaulting her children as a means of winning the power struggle. Moreover, it is important to deconstruct the effect the mothering ideology has on all mothers and reduce the unrealistic expectations of mothers to raise their children in the context of cultural and economic inequality. This reduction would go a long way to alleviate the demoralizing, strainful context many women abide for decades as they raise children and prevent violence toward their children. Using Mead's (1934) significant symbol, Berger and Luckmann's (1966) symbolic universe, Goffman's rehearsals (1959), and Giddens' (1979) theory of the power of social institutions over individuals, I explain why these mothers interpreted the infant's actions negatively and how her irrationality lead to the negative interpretation of infant's behavior. This pivotal point of the challenge warrants further, detailed understanding.

4.2.   A Challenge to the Mother Identity

As previously stated, the mothering ideology provides the initial basis for interpreting the infant's actions, determining the expectations and goals of her role as mother, and how she should behave in order to successfully interact to be a "good" mother and have a "happy" baby that isn't crying.

My theoretical frame of an infant's crying as victim-precipitation is not victim blaming. A baby is cognitively incapable of acting in an intentionally provocative manner. Rather, the initial cause of the negative, misinterpretation is due to a *void of meaning* of the baby's behavior or needs. This void often results in unclear, erroneous meaning and intentions imputed by the mother onto the baby's action. In one case of erroneous, malicious meaning being imposed on a child's action, Goetting (1988) describes a woman who beat her daughter to death as "argu[ing] that the child had refused to mind by continuing to dirty her pants in spite of constant reprimands" (p. 345). Green et al. (1995) corroborate this void in their work on perceptions of crying babies and conclude "the pathways from crying to perception (of actions and intentions) [...] are not direct" (p. 137). A direct pathway occurs only when both actors are able to communicate meaning and cognitively assess a course of action based on their own and the other's meaning. In mother–infant interactions such communication is not possible and the burden of interpreting the baby's actions rests solely with the mother. The interpretation of the meaning by the mother is part of whether she fulfills the identity of "good" mother. If she guesses correctly and the baby stops crying, she is a good mother. If she guesses incorrectly and the crying continues, she is a failing mother. Good mothers know what their babies need.

Applying Mead's (1934) game theory where actors must follow the boundaries set by the generalized other or larger community, the constraints of the mother–child situated transaction have a greater hold over the mother's identity than society in general and may lead to filling the void of meaning incorrectly. When the mother is struggling with her self-perception, she loses her larger perspective on when others think she has crossed the line into irrationality and violent behavior or has lost the ability to put herself in a larger context that would require her to step back. She becomes entrenched in the erroneous meaning and subsequent failing interaction pattern and, increasingly using force, she strives to make her action "work," her guess correct or to achieve the outcome she thinks it will achieve. She *believes* every action or interaction moves her closer to achieving the goal of a happy baby and being a successful mother. These actions can be numerous and come quickly with little time to reflect and reassess the situation. Consequently, the failures come quickly also with little time to reflect on the effort or the overall context. The rapid-fire nature of these attempts erodes rationality and increases emotion. As the mother continues to experience the intensifying, rapidly occurring failures, her frustration and anger increase. When she enters this state, she is irrational and can no longer see the larger context of how her use of force is damaging to her identity of "good mother" and puts the infant at serious risk of injury. She can see only that her action should work and continually tries to make it so. The larger society, or generalized other, will view the transaction as a whole and conclude that she acted irrationally and violently. From the perspective of society, the line crossed can be identified. But the mother cannot see the line due to her myopic entrenchment.

Regardless of inability to communicate meaning, the infant's *actions* are gestures and are taken as direct, significant symbols for whether "good mothering" is being achieved. The inability to assuage the crying or sick baby becomes a significant symbol of failing to meet the internalized social expectations of mothering. This is not as indirect a path as guessing the meaning of actions. The generalized other shares the interpretation of the action of crying by a baby as a significant symbol of whether the mother can soothe its discomfort. "Good" mothers know to calm their child.

An inconsolable baby creates a crisis situation that requires explicit and intensive activities, some of which have been proven previously to be successful (such as walking, patting, holding, etc.). But there are times when babies do not respond in the usual manner and a trend of successful care cannot be established. In these cases, the situation can escalate into a crisis as the activities fail and are repeated with more intensity, often becoming more forceful in an attempt to gain success at consoling or training the baby. As she persists in her attempts, she becomes less rational and more entrenched in actualizing the desired significant symbol – a noncrying, healthy, and trained baby. Scott's (1973) findings on filicide corroborate the loss of irrationality and entrenchment toward meeting the failed expectation with the conclusion that "filicide perpetrators tended to commit the offence when their higher controls were in abeyance and they were acting at so primitive a level that sophisticated motives such as revenge or altruism may be inappropriate [labels]" and, "in a crisis situation, [...] the society itself sets up the specific procedures for situations recognized as involving the risk of a breakdown in reality. The violence of these procedures will be proportional to the seriousness with which the threat is viewed" (Berger & Luckmann, 1966, p. 156).

This implies the emotional escalation of the identity challenge is due to zero thought or cognitive processing precluding an ability to realize her current state of irrational violence. The mother's singularly focus on making her chosen action produce the desired outcome leads to a breakdown in her subjective reality.

This is explained by Mead's (1934) "function of the gesture." According to Mead (1934), "the function of the gesture is to make adjustment possible among the individuals implicated in any given social act with reference to the object or objects with which that act is concerned" (p. 160), for example to stop the crying.

The mother is adjusting her behavior according to her sense of what a "good" mother should do and her interpretation of the significant gesture. In this sense, she is taking the role of the generalized other and significant others on whom she depends or who have control over her. She cognitively processes what she should do or accomplish (such as a baby who is not crying) in an abstract way but her actions have real consequences and she becomes singularly focused. Paraphrasing Mead (1934, p. 175), once the mother arouses in herself the expectations of mothering, she gets self-conscious, [...] she takes the attitude of the other, and tries to determine what the outcome of her efforts should be. Then she adjusts her behavior in a way that she believes will achieve that outcome. But an effective adjustment, at a minimum, requires a correct interpretation of the infant's need. Her adjustments are based on a guessing game as she continually or repeatedly fails to assuage the crying. Yet, she is compelled by the challenge to her identity to continue acting toward achieving the outcome. By acting, she assumes responsibility for this situation and determination. As further stated by Mead, "When a person acts, they are affirming the significance of the object or symbol. With this affirmation, they are accepting responsibility for the meaning they subscribe to the object or context and they own their role in the fulfillment of the required outcome" (p. 175).

Furthermore, by continuing the engagement, she is upholding the social construction of the normative expectation that it must be the mother who attends the child (Hays, 1996). Friedman et al. (2005) critically analyzed 39 studies on neonaticide, infanticide, and filicide and find that the perpetrating mothers have the common trait of "having primary responsibility" (p. 1581). And, although the mothering ideology compels her to act, this trait is reaffirmed when the mother takes responsibility for the context by continuing to act. This circularity of compulsion illustrates the entrenchment of mothering.

While Mead's theory of significant symbols fits well here, it assumes the generalized other is socially organized — "in so far as the individual arouses in [her] self the attitudes of the others, there arises an *organized* group of responses" (p. 175). As previously discussed, parenting, particularly mothering, is socially disorganized at the social or generalized other level and increasingly anomic partly due to the child rearing industry. Women socialized into this role do not receive an organized group of responses for acting toward an inconsolable baby. The responses they receive and internalize *appear* to be organized based on the belief that the actions will assuage the crying and that a "good mother" naturally knows what her baby wants. The child-rearing experts and media (see Hays, 1996) assume this organization and proscribe recipes of action. But in reality, the broad ideals appear successful only when the mother is able to achieve the expectations in a short amount of time. When achievement requires more time and intensive care, the proscriptions start failing. For those who represent the generalized other, when the proscribed actions fail, it is because the mother is not doing something correctly or that she does not have good parenting skills, rather than the experts admitting or realizing their proscriptions are also based on a guessing game. The attempts lead to a feedback loop where the generalized other (i.e., mothering ideology) produces crises with unrealistic expectations that, in turn, create untested, unclear social proscriptions for action and guiding principles. Once implemented and failed, a mother's action is judged negatively by her internalized, generalized other or the mothering ideology. This self-feeding situation is a major force affecting when mothers are able to reflectively monitor and intelligently reflect on the current course of action. The more the mother struggles with this force, the more emotion work is required. The emotion work "batters" and demoralizes her to a point where she no longer reflects and evaluates her current actions and the force with which she applies them. The interaction a mother has with her infant can start as instrumental, such as comforting a crying baby in order to have a happy baby, but becomes transmuted into a goal itself — getting the baby to stop crying becomes the goal with a loss of sight of the original purpose, that is, raising a happy, healthy child, as the mother becomes obsessed with stopping the crying. At this point, she has stopped monitoring herself and is unable to intelligently reflect on her and the baby's actions.

4.3.   Reflexive Monitoring/Reflective Intelligence and Emotion Work

Mothering requires conceiving a wide range of possible options and responses. Having this ability enables her to effectively process the situation (Fisk & Taylor, 2013), understand it, and manage her emotions. The pivotal point between no injury and risk of severe injury is very likely the mother being able to catch herself, figuratively stepping back, and think about her interaction with her baby. This involves two tandem steps: one, the mother chronically monitoring her behavior and two, realizing when she needs to think about and perhaps change her actions. I explain these steps using reflexive monitoring (Giddens, 1979) and reflective intelligence (Mead, 1934) as the correlated processes of "stepping back" from a high-emotion, stressful situation to a rational reevaluation of one's course of action.

According to Giddens (1979), "human beings reflexively monitor their conduct via the knowledge they have of the circumstances of their activity" (p. 254) including "the monitoring of the setting of interaction, and not just the behavior of the particular actors taken separately" (p. 57). Reflexive monitoring is a continuous judging of whether a course of action is getting the desired result and is based on knowledge that is a "coding" system for when something is or is not working. This can range from nonconscious awareness to being fully conscious of failing actions. Reactivity and monitoring are a desire to end a stressful or painful situation. If the actor's actions are not working, reflexive monitoring detects this and reflective intelligence is prompted as a process of examining what is being done, what was done in the past, suggestions or ideas from the stock of knowledge or generalized other, creativity, and mental rehearsals for what to do next. Reflective intelligence (Mead, 1934) is accessing more deeply the stock of knowledge in a person's mind and analyzing the current course of action in light of all known possibilities. Put differently, reflective intelligence is using the mind. Mead sees the mind as a "great cooperative community process" [...] that is the "interplay of gesture in form of significant signals" (pp. 188–189). The interplay requires rational conduct so that "the individual should thus take an objective, impersonal attitude toward himself" (p. 138). By this application, the mother experiences herself as such, not directly, but only indirectly, from the particular standpoints of other individual members of the same social group, or from the *generalized* standpoint of the social group as a whole to which she belongs. In other words, the mother becomes an object to herself only by taking the attitudes of other individuals, that is, the stock of knowledge from the generalized other, toward herself within a social environment of experience and behavior in which both she and the baby are involved.

For mothers, this stock of knowledge is the mothering ideology and the vast array of "expert-driven" media. The continual reflexive monitoring is due to the prominent mother identity that creates an ever-present awareness of the social expectations for being a "good mother." Reflective intelligence is aroused when the monitoring detects something deviant or when the first significant symbol of unmet social expectations of mothering is detected. A crying baby makes the goal of assuaging discomfort salient and detected. The mother is compelled to act. In this context, the identity of mothering is ever-present and being monitored by her. This demonstrates the power of the social institution or social expectations over the mother. The unyielding demands of the identity continuously compel her even if the baby's behavior changes from unhappy to happy. For prominent identities such as the mother role, as soon as one expectation is met, another immediately arises.

Impression management (Goffman, 1959) of a mother, even unto herself, is never-ending all the while she is adjusting according to important, salient social expectations. How easily adjusted and perceptive the monitoring is depends on her self-esteem or successful rehearsals with the infant. If rehearsals have been successful in meeting the social expectations, she is not aroused toward intensive reflective intelligence nor experiences the onset of stress and is more resilient to the challenge. In these cases, the evaluation of the interactions does not require adjustments in the management of behavior. However, if rehearsals have been unsuccessful, the monitoring may immediately put the mother into an emotional state – a carryover or residue of the prior, failed rehearsals. Here, there is a cumulative effect that leaves the mother exhausted, less capable of monitoring, and more likely to respond violently. Being able to step back from this state requires the additional work of keeping her emotions in check. As pointed out by Giddens (1979) there is a "stratification model of action [that] emphasizes intentionality of an action as a process" (p. 56). He asserts that intentionality is a routine feature of human behavior and to act purposefully toward rationality is to have an uncommon degree of mental application. This is reflective intelligence – conscientiously focusing on a salient issue and intentionally, mindfully acting toward it. Such mindfulness requires emotion work.

According to Hochschild (1989), emotion work is the process of evoking, suppressing, or otherwise managing feelings. Emotion work for mothers attempting to meet the expectations of the role requires impression management (Goffman, 1959) to herself and others that she is suppressing any feelings of frustration and anger. Maushart (1999) calls this "masking" and argues that the socially required suppression of feelings masks the reality of mothering and "a woman who catches sight of herself in the mirror – as it were, unmasked – sees a very different picture [from the one she is trying to portray]. And the message is clear: she is a failure" (p. 8).

To fail to mask her true feelings of frustration and anger is an egregious violation of mothering norms since these expressions are interpreted as not having loving feelings toward her baby. "A person incapable of masking her true feelings is often regarded [by others] as immature, sick, or both. To a very considerable degree, what we call self-control depends on our ability to 'mask', to deny and repress what we experience" (Maushart, 1999, p. 1).

The structural pressures of emotion work eventually alienate the person from their own feelings. Such alienation can include losing the ability to sympathize and care for others but also includes not caring about one's self. As fatigue increases, the ability to care decreases. The periods between failed or almost-failed interactions with the infants require energy and time. A lack of success or the amount of effort required to achieve success chronically increases fatigue. The mother becomes less able to do the emotion work required to rationally, intelligently reflect. Consequently, emotion work is not always successful and frustration is not checked. At this point, the mother is in a high state of arousal. Such fatigue is not unknown to mothers. Data from my ongoing survey of expectations of mothering show that 51% of mothers in the sample experience constant fatigue and 61% report they wake up exhausted (Smithey, 2018). The following statements from mothers in my qualitative interviews include words and phrases such as "exhausted," "stressed," and "fatigued" to demonstrate the level of fatigue at which they are functioning.

> I was exhausted all the time. My marriage was very stressful to me and my baby took up a lot of my time and energy.

> I was always irritable and stressed. My husband did not understand that.

One mother revealed that she was masking her stress and fatigue.

> I was alone and really stressed. I stayed to myself. I am very private. I didn't want anyone to see me the way I was (meaning stressed and fatigued).

Three mothers describe how the lack of sleep contributed to the fatigue and, in one case, the foregoing of sleep and meals to deal with the crying baby.

> I was very fatigued toward the end of my pregnancy and the lack of sleep after he was born made it worse.

> I didn't sleep much because I was always listening for the baby to cry. I didn't want him to cry a lot. And I forgot to eat. He was my fourth child and was born just 9 months after my last one.

> I was always tired and I got very little sleep. I was tired when he
> was born, you know, from being pregnant and all that, then he
> was born and that made everything worse.

As these data show, many mothers are chronically exhausted which may
affect their ability to intellectually work out their stressful interactions with the
infant. In addition to the fatigue, the stress of a crying baby, the effort put into
emotion work, and other predispositional factors impede her ability to reflexively monitor. She is experiencing "monitoring overload" as her environment
demands she conquer multiple failing goals – overdue bills, no food, needed
medicine, no diapers, a failing marriage or abusive boyfriend or husband, and a
failing sense of self due to low self-esteem. At any time, this overload can leave
her believing she is a *complete* failure. Scott (1973), concludes that "the impulse
(to kill) may be transferred to the child from another cause [...] there are under-
lying frustrations." Oberman (2003) finds also that infanticide does not occur
solely because of a mother's mental impairment but is a combination of the
mother's vulnerable mental status and other predispositional factors that shape
the context in which she is expected to parent.

If the mother's socialization and other interpersonal relationship have damaged her (Crimmins et al., 1997), this also reduces her ability to reflexively monitor. The mothering role is secondary socialization during which she learns the
ideologically driven expectations for the role of mothering. But secondary socialization is problematic for women who were damaged during primary socialization during which you learn the basics of humanity such as sympathy and
empathy. With primary preceding secondary socialization, persons who had negative, failed life experiences have an already formed self that persists despite the
secondary socialization content correcting or contradicting it. In these instances,
the mother is incapable of recalling or imagining positive solutions or outcomes
of interpersonal actions that may help her manage her emotions better and there
may be "no social self or reference point from which to implement the secondary
socialization content" (Berger & Luckmann, 1966, p. 140). In other words, there
is no healthy self with whom to intelligently reflect.

Moreover, there is little time to work out the conversation. Mothers
need time to check their emotions, reflect, and enact reflective intelligence.
Experiencing any emotional reward while interacting with the infant requires the
skills to define interpersonal relationships as rewarding and some length of time
between the infant's episodes of discomfort. Experiences of emotional reward
are important because they reenergize and diminish the fatiguing, chronic failure
of infant care that leads to irrationality. Hays (1996) cites several mothers in
her study who told her that the quality of the time they spend with their
children increases when they have a chance to be away from them for part of
the day. This is especially true for ill or difficult to train infants. These factors
are interactive and self-feeding causing chronic fatigue and make mothering
more emotionally draining and labor-intensive than usual, especially if the baby
is unwanted.

The entirety of the failing situation is a significant challenge for her. Being able to reflect intelligently via the mothering ideology assumes rational conduct. This ability is inverse to fatigue and emotion work. When a mother is attempting to reconcile the negative feelings she is experiencing with the feeling she has been socialized to expect to feel according to the romanticized picture of mothering and the expected ability to assuage crying, she is experiencing strain. The more she fails at this reconciliation, the more interpersonal strain she feels. This conflict is particularly more stressful and chronic for women than men (Broidy & Agnew, 1997) due to their gendered socialization to nurture and care for others. The goal of a woman's interpersonal relationships being the happiness and approval by others is magnified by the mothering ideology making this objective even more important for mothers caring for their children. The chronic strain becomes suffering and she is operating in a demoralized state. Her ability to intelligently reflect or act rationally is greatly compromised and reduced. The generalized other looms large and blurs an objective evaluation of her current context. Her identity as a "good mother" and overall character is seriously challenged as she continues to view her actions as failing.

The anomic character of the mothering ideology contributes to the self-questioning of her ability. It makes the socialization into the role mother "artificial" and the identity even more susceptible to challenges, "not because [it is] taken for granted or apprehended as less than real [...] but because ideology restricts and distorts the situation and circumstances of the [mother's] actions making it less [internalized] and therefore more subject to displacement" (Berger & Luckmann, 1967, p. 148).

"Reflective" is having a conversation with the one's self about the ideology as it is interpreted within one's own mind (Berger & Luckmann, 1966, p. 140). If the reference point is anomic, that is, unclear, lacking guiding principles, or contradictory, there is not a generalized other (Mead, 1934) or macroscopic universe (Berger & Luckmann, 1966) to mediate the conversation she has with herself between what she is doing and what she should be doing to achieve the outcomes of a "good" mother. The content for the conversation itself is problematic.

How wanted the child affects reflexive monitoring. As discussed in Chapter 2, the less the child is wanted mediates the higher the likelihood of injury (see Table 4.2). Conversely, the more the child is wanted, the greater the degree of reflexive monitoring that can trigger reflective intelligence. Wanting or planning the baby is also an intervening variable that may produce a stronger investment in "good mothering." In this case, the emotion work of being a mother can begin before the conception of the fetus. Here, while arguably unrealistic or naively done, the ability to meet the expectations of mothering begins well before the reality of mothering occurs. This investment and emotional desire may be an intervening variable between the infliction of a lethal injury and "catching oneself." Unfortunately, this ideal case does not fit most pregnancies. Planning a pregnancy is a strong indicator of wanting a child. The data from my survey research show that two-thirds of mothers had not planned to become pregnant. As discussed in Chapter 2, other studies find similar results. While a portion of the unplanned pregnancies may result in a wanted baby, it is probable

Table 4.2. Wantedness and Planning Affecting Likelihood of Reflexive Monitoring and Reflective Intelligence.

Pregnancy	Wanted	Unwanted
Planned	Highest likelihood of reflexive monitoring and reflective intelligence	Moderate-to-low likelihood of reflexive monitoring and reflective intelligence
Unplanned	Moderate-to-high likelihood of reflexive monitoring and reflective intelligence	Lowest likelihood of reflexive monitoring and reflective intelligence

that a larger portion of unplanned pregnancies result in unwantedness. Violent episodes toward an unwanted baby take on a dimension of instrumental violence to eliminate an unwanted child (Scott, 1973). On some level, the mother does not want the child and may be more likely to strike out against this circumstance.

This is the context of crisis under which a lethal injury is most likely. Child abuse researchers and criminal justice and social services workers refer to assaults under these conditions as "losing it." This phrase assumes the conditions under which mothers act are conducive to rationality and that the suffering, chronic emotion work experience by the assailing mothers is nonexistent or constant across all mothers. Yet, many mothers have an unspoken understanding of just how easily or close they have come to losing it. In fact, the difference between those who injure their children and those who do not may be more precarious than we care to admit. This precariousness makes us all vulnerable to "losing it" and assaulting someone, including our own children.

It is in this inhibiting environment that society makes itself known by pressuring mothers into achieving certain outcomes and repeating actions toward the child that are not working. The mother is trapped and cannot escape this intense, emotion-laden task of assuaging a seemingly inconsolable baby. Society expects her to remain in the intensifying context until she succeeds. Good mothers do not walk away from their crying babies.

Chapter 5

A Crying Baby and the Inability to Escape

What was I supposed to do? Just walk out the door and never come back? Who was gonna let me do that? Who would think THAT'S OK?

In this chapter, I make the second part of my sociological argument by continuing the stages of the situation transaction of infanticide and explaining the mother's inability to escape the intense, overwhelming situation of managing an unhappy baby in the context of economic and cultural inequality. Due to gender role socialization, females internalize the obligation that they must be the one to care for their infant (Hays, 1996) when no one else is willing or no other resource is available. Exasperation and desperation result in physical force as the mother tries to restore order and gain compliance with the social expectations of her baby being a "happy" baby, that is, not crying, being healthy, and successful feeding, sleeping, and potty training. I apply Gidden's (1984) theory of power of social institutions over individuals to explain the increasing exasperation and desperation due to an inability to escape the stressful context.

The mother becoming more forceful in an attempt to restore order is due to an inability to escape the intense, overwhelming situation of managing a crying baby. The baby's crying continues to be interpreted by the mother as noncompliance with her efforts to meet the goals of mothering ideology. Exasperation and desperation become physical force as the mother tries to restore order and gain compliance. The heightened emotions escalate into a lethal, but often unintended, injury. Here the progression from rationality to emotionally "losing it" overwhelms and negates the ability to reflexively monitor and reflectively apply intelligent problem solving (Berger & Luckmann, 1966; Mead, 1934). This progression is the result of a combination of the stress and suffering of mothering which sometimes includes substance use as a coping mechanism, social isolation, the arousal of violence, and the belief that asking for help is symbolic of a bad mother.

5.1. Suffering and a Poor Quality of Life

As discussed previously, the mothering ideology produces cultural inequality in the childcare division of labor, reduces economic success and participation, and demoralizes women as they attempt to meet the unrealistic, anomic expectations of mothering, and economically and culturally survive the gendered expectations of work and family. Lang (2005) describes this as "suffering" — a term often upheld by religious beliefs as virtuous for women and underscores the centrality of the mother identity for women.

> The historical existence of women who injure or kill their children suggests that motherhood can [...] be experienced as negative suffering. [It is] in contrast to the positive suffering women are taught to expect (p. 116).

The suffering mothers experience while raising children causes a reduced quality of life or may exacerbate an already poor quality of life. Besides depression and fatigue, women often cope by sacrificing their own wants and needs. Culturally, maternal sacrifice is mandated (Cutrona, 1984; LaRossa, 1986; Wandersman, Wandersman, & Kahn, 1980). Achieving the status of "good" mother requires a willingness to make personal sacrifices, follow "expert-driven" knowledge (Hays, 1996), and have a significant nurturing ability. Additionally, belief in maternal instinct mandates sacrifice. Mothers are expected to "naturally" put children above all else − including their own emotional and physical health. The status of mothering often is seen not only as the ultimate, but even as the only, fulfillment of womanhood. Fear of failing to achieve generates great negative affect.

The characteristics and outcomes of suffering include loss of personal time, sleep, needed personal items, leisure activity, and love. For example, Hays (1996) describes mothering as emotionally draining, labor intensive, and unappreciated. Hochschild (1989, 1997) writes extensively on the imbalance of time demands, mothers managing childcare while being a time-and-motion expert that requires meeting often conflicting schedules for herself and her children, and loss of personal or leisure time. The US Department of Labor data (2015) show that mothers, compared to fathers, are still spending an extra 15.5 hours a month on housework and an extra 13.69 hours a month on childcare. Combined, this results in 14.6 24-hour days a year more than fathers. These circumstances culminate in a reduced quality of life due to little or no time for mothers to care for themselves.

A lack of economic resources contributes to this suffering. Mothers without economic resources, especially single mothers, experience chronic despair and hopelessness as they strive to gather food, medicine, and other needed goods. This frequently includes sacrificing the needed material goods for self-care and personal pleasures. Interactively, the lack of economic and social resources for raising a child are tantamount to being a victim of unrealistic circumstances that chronically, emotionally "batter" a woman as she attempts to assuage the discomfort, illness, and hunger of children with insufficient funds.

Besides loss of help and love due to intimate partner violence, mothers also sacrifice loss of love from intimate partners due to child-rearing time demands and expectations. These demands reduce opportunity for intimacy and become a chronic condition of the mother not experiencing love. This loss of love is not immediately compensated by love from the infant. While many mothers feel and express love toward their infant, the love is not automatically reciprocated. The intangibility of the reward of child rearing is due to an imbalance in the reciprocity norm of love. Mothers experience this imbalance for two or three years

(Gelles, 1978; Rodriguez & Smithey, 1999) until the child can express loving feelings or actions toward the mother. LaRossa (1986) refers to infants and children as "sponges" that lack the cognitive ability to reciprocate yet rapidly soak up the benefits of the actions of their mother. This does not suggest that infants intentionally fail to give back, their cognitive and physiological lack of development required for their physiological survival create an insatiability that cannot be fulfilled for more than a short period of time. Feeling loved by an infant requires interpreting their actions in a positive manner – something that is unlikely to occur when the infant is crying, difficult to train, or unwanted. Mothers need love and this unfulfilled need due to marital sacrifice and unreciprocated love from their baby produces suffering that has the ability to impair judgment. This is evident in the following excerpt from an intensive interview in which the mother's desire for love came at the expense of her infant's life as when she chose intimate love over her child.

> [Her new boyfriend] didn't want my little boy in the picture at all. And then he calls on the phone and says I need you to come over to my mom's house and I said I can't go. [...] I had my little girl sick, and then I had my little boy asleep at this time. He said I want you to come over here and I said I'm sorry I can't go 'cause I got, I got my little kids here, you know, my little girl's getting well and my little boy's asleep right now and I can't, no I can't go right now. And then I don't have no transportation, and I gotta go on the bus, you know, over there and it would've took so long and then to carry two kids, a stroller and so much, it's, it's a lot, you know, so um, he says well if you love me enough you'll come over here. (She took her daughter with her and left the infant unattended and did not return for eleven days. The autopsy report estimated the infant died within forty-eight hours.)

While the stress and suffering is chronic and intense, the quality of life for many mothers may be mediated by their belief in the ideology of mothering and their socioeconomic status. A mother who believes strongly in the ideology would have the stamina and devotion to achieving the goal of "good mother" regardless of how unclear or difficult the expectations. Her determination can yield more dedicated thought and energy to finding solutions or doing the emotion work required to convince herself that she has done a good job, is a good mother, and that mothering is rewarding. The emotion work of interpreting infant behavior as loving includes redefining crying and other difficult childcare tasks as temporary or "stages" through which the baby is going. To achieve this, mothers look to a short-term future when the baby has "outgrown" this stage and is capable of doing new things that may be more readily interpreted as fun. Having the capacity to do this emotion work leads to a greater (and sooner) arousal prompting reflective intelligence resulting in a greater level of sustained rationality.

But belief and commitment to mothering ideology succeeds only to a point. The reflective monitoring and reflexive intelligence are "rehearsals" in her head regarding how to best achieve the desired outcome — a noncrying, happy baby. Even with commitment and devotion to the infant, each subsequent rehearsal or attempt at making the baby happy taxes her emotion work and may shorten her stamina and devotion. If the rehearsals become too frequent, at some point her emotions will turn in a negative direction as she intellectually and emotionally start interpreting the outcomes as those of a failing mother.

The chronic emotion work of stepping-back, regardless of her dedication, is a form of suffering that reduces the ability to reflexively monitor and reflect intelligently and contributes to a loss of identity as a good mother. And under the conditions of sacrificing self-care, the mother's strength and sense of self fades. In her work on the cultural contradictions of motherhood, Hays (1996) finds that many stay-at-home moms experience the "exhaustion of muting the demands of children all day and experience a loss of self" (p. 64). Wall (2001) finds similar conclusions and describes many mothers as "talking [...] of feeling inadequate in the face of a continually crying baby and of a loss of personal identity as their whole world becomes centered on a baby" (p. 598). This centering is due to the invasion or imposition of the baby into the mother's daily life. The invasion can precede or occur simultaneously with suffering. The majority of mothers report the suffering as being overwhelmed by childcare (Crandall et al., 2006).

Another mitigating factor is the extent to which the child is wanted. The child being wanted to some degree also can mitigate suffering and the likelihood of injury. Whether the child was planned affects the degree of the baby's invasion into the mother's well-being. Unwantedness directly fuels the suffering, whether present during the pregnancy or occurs after the birth and experiencing the reality of parenting. Unwantedness during the pregnancy can be early onset suffering and invasion depending on how medically complicated the pregnancy and feelings of being trapped and unable to escape the situation. Postnatal onset of unwantedness and suffering can be from the realization that having and raising a child is different from the romanticized ideals that are gender socialized. This is a direct, pervasive invasion of the infant into the mother's life.

A lack of support and economic resources, living in adverse conditions, and the other factors and conditions described thus far become tantamount to victimization of the mother by the anomic, unrealistic expectations of parenting. The unfulfilled expectations continuously emotionally batter a woman who must assuage the discomfort and hunger of children in addition to the normal, immediate stressors and physical demands of child rearing. This battering consists of a lack of freedom and reduced economic opportunity, which increases the likelihood that she cannot escape chronic, stressful childrearing. For women who are in absolute poverty, having no economic resources makes it nearly impossible to escape, even temporarily (Belknap, 1996). This can push women into a situation where instrumental or expressive violence is the outcome. As a form of instrumental violence, the option to eliminate the child via murder may be seen as the only way out of the chronic "battering" of childrearing with no resources. As expressive violence the lethal violence is the result of pent-up emotions due to unfulfilled expectations or what was previously described as "losing it."

Mothers can experience the same type of battering stress from childrearing in a dual-parent family when economic resources may not be as low as that of single mothers, but the intrafamilial, cultural gender inequality is the same. For dual-parent patriarchal families, there is often only one person responsible for housework and childcare. In these cases, the mother does all the microlevel decision-making of childcare and housework but does not have control over the use and allocation of money and time (Hays, 1996; Hochschild, 1989, 1997). For low-income families, decision-making power is very low due to economic deprivation and stressful living conditions that severely restrict her options. In either of these contexts, the "decisions" are made for her rendering a false impression that mothers in dual-parent families have the power to make resource decisions regarding house and childcare. As stated by Lang (2005),

> [Models of liberty presume women] will become the suffering imposed by having and rearing children [...] the woman is Foucault's "docile body" constructed to act and produce as the state decides. The concern is not a failure to grant mothers liberty to choose to suffer [...] but rather a failure to grant mothers the liberty to choose not to suffer [...] women are subjected to a culturally powerful myth that disables the liberty to choose (pp. 126, 128).

To restate, there is a societal expectation or presumption that women are "willing" to suffer when in reality women are subjected to a culturally powerful myth that disables the liberty to choose. Infanticide is the most extreme proof of the fact that not all women willingly choose the suffering motherhood entails. Or as Morrissey (2003) and Gartner and McCarthy (2006) put it, these mothers are both violent and agentic. Whether these women are deemed irrational or empowered to "strike back" against the unrealistic, anomic norms of mothering, the fact remains that they have little power to change the preexisting state of affairs of the social institution of the family and parenting (Giddens 1979,1984). Often the patriarchal powers of society deem women's behavior as irrational as a means to control them toward conformity of the expected gender roles.

Suffering and the accompanying powerlessness and chronic fatigue keep the mother in a demoralized state that transcends any immediate context of interaction. Not only does she perceived herself as failing to meet the norms of good mothering, she comes to view herself as a bad mother with no options to change the preexisting state of affairs that are the institutionalized social structures of parenting. Without any options, some suffering mothers turn to substance use to cope.

5.2. Substance Use and Abuse

Some mothers use substances to block the pain caused by the chronic and some-times acute suffering. Five mothers interviewed report using alcohol and mari-juana on a regular basis after the infant was born.

> We drank a lot. I just needed a break. Somebody always remained intelligent. You know, with the kids around and all.

> I didn't realize that, I knew I was drinking too much and one time I wound up in the hospital and that made me snap towards (think about) my daughter because she made me aware I was drinking too much. Really, all I drank was wine coolers. I didn't use drugs, I can't stand needles.

> I was smoking weed when I got a chance [...] I never smoked around the kids. That was the hardest (drug) I did. Smoked just on the weekends.

The inability to escape legally can result in escaping illegally (Agnew, 1992). The negative stimuli of the environment lead to negative effect, such as fear, despair, disappointment, depression, and anger (p. 58) and substances are used to alleviate the stress and manage the negative effect. Unfortunately, although the substance abuse may temporarily alleviate the stress experienced by mothers, the mothers I interviewed report that sometimes the effects of alcohol impaired the mother's ability to reflexively monitor. They report heightened aggression by the mother due misinterpretation of the infant's actions. Other studies find simi-larly and indicate that reduced inhibition, inability to assess one's own behavior, increased impulsivity, and threats to personal self are significant intervening variables between alcohol consumption and increased levels of aggression (Cherek & Steinberg, 1987; Crandall et al., 2006; Gelles & Straus, 1988; Mayfield, 1976; Rimm, Briddell, Zimmerman, & Caddy, 1981; Sobell & Sobell, 1975; Zeichner & Pihl, 1979). Alcohol use has an intervening relationship with stress and infant homicide in two ways. In one way, its use may result in a more difficult baby to manage. Alcohol and drug abuse during pregnancy has been linked to atypically ill newborns (Chasnoff, Hatcher, & Burns, 1982; Gonzales & Campbell, 1994). Another source of stressful child-rearing comes from drug abuse during pregnancy leading to atypically ill newborns, typically described as irritability, poor feeding patterns, and irregular sleep patterns (Chasnoff et al., 1982). The resulting higher, abnormal levels of difficulty of car-ing for infants would further increase the likelihood of the mother being aggres-sive toward the infant.

The second effect stems from the impaired judgment while interacting with the infant. Altered perception of self and others, increased impulsivity and threats to personal self have been cited as significant intervening variables between alcohol consumption and levels of aggression (Cherek & Steinberg, 1987; Crandall et al., 2006; Gelles & Straus, 1988; Rimm et al., 1981). For example, one mother described how a friend intervened while she was disciplining her infant under the influence of alcohol,

> I would hit her on the butt, hit her in the shoulders, my friend would tell me don't hit her like that, it's wrong, in other words I was beating her, as I had a drinking problem, and I would take out all my anger at her.

In another more serious case, the mother's use of cocaine directly affected interaction with the infant and contributed to his death.

> The baby started crying. I was smoking crack. The baby wouldn't stop crying so I kept on hitting him. I didn't realize I was hitting him so hard. (The infant died from abdomen trauma).

The physical toll of the substance use, the chronic emotion work, and lack of economic resources lead to chronic fatigue and the inability to meet the expectations of mothering become more pronounced in the mother's mind. The suffering becomes oppressive and the cultural inequality motivates the mother toward violence as the intangible, abstract reward of childcare escapes or dissipates as she strives to keep her baby "happy."

Consequently, the situated context of infant homicide is two persons – a mother and her infant – who are acting from a survival standpoint, although from very different forces, one social and the other natural. Under these conditions, the stress, mitigated by substance abuse or other deviant behaviors, negatively affects her ability to reflexively monitor as the intense behavioral exchange escalates toward a fatal injury of the infant. And neither of them can escape.

5.3. The Inability to Escape

Without the ever-present predispositions discussed so far, the cultural inequality and subsequent stress are sufficient to impede effective, reflexive intelligence as is demonstrated by child abuse in all socioeconomic statuses (Straus & Gelles, 1990). While demoralization is emotional entrapment, the mothering ideology also physically traps mothers. Stepping back, discussed thus far as a mental exercise, can also consist of physically removing oneself from the stressful situation. In this case, the mother has done the emotion work required to reflect on the interaction and developed another course of action – getting away from the crying baby. Interview excerpts already presented include phrases such as "I was stuck," "I just wanted to go," and "I shut myself in my room" showing that while reflecting on their situation, the mothers realized they needed to physically remove themselves from the crying baby but were unable to because of fear of possible social and criminal justice sanctions.

A mothering taking a short break in an attempt to calm herself demonstrates self-control. Usually short breaks involve staying within hearing distance of the baby but sometimes they include complete sensory removal from the situation, such as going outside after making sure the crying baby is safe and secure. Still, these breaks carry some safety risk even when taken for just a minute. The length of time a mother removes herself from a crying baby has varying consequences, especially if the baby is unsafe or found unsupervised. Brief, nearby reprieves can be viewed as an intelligent, self-aware step. Longer breaks are not viewed in this manner and have more serious safety consequences that can include criminal charges and legal removal of the child from the mother's care. All states have laws that punish persons for leaving children unattended, even for a few minutes. For low socioeconomic status mothers these laws are salient as they interact with social support services, school officials, neighbors, and family. Such services often require or automatically implement supervision of home and child activities as a condition of receiving the service. Working and middle-class mothers have more economic resources to use daycare or hire sitters but this requires making arrangements that often have a degree of uncertainty − such as the child becoming sick or the money being needed for other expenses − and may not be immediately available.

Using social support networks for scheduled breaks or to help when the mother is overly stressed usually consists of asking a friend or family member to come over or babysit or expending economic resources on paid childcare. When the mother cannot get this support, she has no choice but to stay with or return to the situation. The mothering ideology has rendered her powerless to physically escape. No other action appears as an option because constraint is deeply ingrained in the mothering ideology due to societal belief in "maternal attachment" − that mothers are biologically driven to automatically love, nurture, and protect their children above all else. Due to this pervasive cultural belief, mothers are allowed only to have and express positive feelings toward their children. The expression of negative feelings and unhappiness toward your children is an egregious violation of motherhood norms.

5.4.   Social Isolation

Social isolation is part of the inability to escape and increases significantly the likelihood of injurious assault and lethality (Smith-Lovin & McPherson, 1993). "Escaping" can be in the literal form of being able to remove oneself from an environment. But for parenting, "escaping" the escalating demands and tension from the unmet norms of the motherhood ideology can mean turning to another person for reflexive intelligence and help. Socially isolated mothers do not have benefits of a support person and experiences a limited ability to escape the actions of the infant that symbolize failure. When a stressed mother turns to a support person, that mother is seeking rationality and guardianship. This may be the last vestige of recognition that she is entering "survival mode" and is on the brink of total loss of rational understanding. Without a means to alleviate her strainful social and economic conditions, she may transfer blame to visible and vulnerable targets in the immediate environment and retaliate against those targets (Bernard, 1990), including infants. As discussed earlier, many well-intending friends and family members who have given support are soon depleted of goodwill, as the multitude of needs of these mothers becomes a stressful, daily event that results in adverse living conditions.

Mothers who are trapped and isolated in these conditions are likely to be thought of as single. But the negative impact of isolation is as applicable to dual-parent families as much as it is to single mothers. Overwhelmingly, mothers do the majority of house care and childcare regardless of whether the father is present. Their presence does not automatically mean the mother is getting help and emotional support. In fact, fathers or male partners often increase her work-load, stress, emotional fatigue, and demoralization. Research on dual-parent families demonstrates that many women who are "dual-parenting" are in fact single-parenting (Hays, 1996; Hochschild, 1989; Lindsey, 2005; Warner, 2005) and often in the context of an antagonistic husband or boyfriend (Smithey, 1998). The only tangible difference relative to single mothers is that there may be increased economic resources and there may be potential for assistance when there are scheduling conflicts, although negotiating schedules is often stressful.

The baby is also more vulnerable to harm due to social isolation where there are no other capable guardians to intervene and stop an escalation of violence. In a review of studies of child homicide in Europe, Stroud (2008) concludes that child homicide occurred in the context of the perpetrator being isolated, deprived of meaningful, reciprocal interaction, and "[having] no close friends [...] there was no one to mediate between the individual, their stress, and mental health and the child" (p. 496).

Economic inequality of women is another significant contributor to the isola-tion of mothers who then becoming trapped in intensive behavioral and emo-tional exchanges with inconsolable infants. Not having economic resources makes it nearly impossible for a distressed, exhausted mother to escape, even temporarily, from the source of their stress (Jensen, 2001). Violence is often the result when women see no way out. It becomes an option for dramatically taking control of the context in which they find themselves. And asking for help carries the risk of being viewed as a bad or incapable mother.

5.5. The Humiliation of Asking for Help

The stress of an inability to escape can be exacerbated by the act of asking for help. This is true in a capitalist society where strength and competitiveness are highly regarded and rewarded. The interactional environment of capitalism is competitive and persons socialized in this environment learn that asking for help is a sign of weakness producing the perception that you cannot do what is expected. This cultural belief requires that mothers continually match the managed impressions of other mothers who may also be masking their suffering and entrapment. Additionally, people see *offering help* as judgmental and intrusive because the offer itself symbolizes that the person offering it perceives the recipient as incapable. Consequently, asking for help and offering help both symbolize failure on the part of the person in need. Stanton and Skipworth's (2005) study of mothers finds this to be the case for mothers who relayed "accounts of reluctance to ask for help related to perceived negative judgment of help-seeking" (p. 160).

Yet, many desperate mothers ask for help despite the negative judgment and humiliation. Stroud (2008) studied 68 mothers who committed infanticide and finds that over one-third sought help. Sandy Simpson, a psychiatrist who has worked with infanticidal mothers, reports,

> one strong theme that came through the research was of the need for help and *a sense of risk in getting help.* The risk is that if I tell it like I fear it may be, people will think I'm not fit to be a parent (Hewitson, 2000, p. 2).

The courageous attempts at asking someone for help do not always produce the needed result. I find that when some of the mothers interviewed asked for help, her family members were unwilling or unable to assist with caring for the infant. For example,

> Even before things happened (events leading up to the death of the infant), I asked my own family for help and they turned me down.

> When I wanted some help, nobody would help me.

> They would babysit, [...] really it depends on when I needed to go somewhere. This was so I could rest. Or they'd go shopping for me. But this only lasted about a year. Then they was tired of it all.

> Mom was very understanding. She would try to be there for me, but she was already raising my sister's kids.

> My mom and sister would help me for a while but then stopped.

> A week before [the baby] died, I told my neighbor he was very difficult and driving me nuts, that his crying is driving me crazy. I was weak and wanted her to get me an appointment at the hospital. [The neighbor did not respond].

> My mom didn't like my boyfriend [the baby's father] so I didn't ask her for much so I wouldn't have to hear [her complaining about him].

Asking for help despite the negative judgment and humiliation indicates a level of desperateness preceding the fatal exchange and affects the ability to rationally follow through on possible options. The following story of a mother calling for help a few days before the infanticide illustrates how desperation can impede rational action.

> I had called this agency one time in [city name] and I had told, it was like I was seeking for help, you know, and I was crying on the phone telling this lady, look, I need some, I need some help here, you know, because I can't attend to my little boy, I can't attend to him, I need some help, I need to do something, you know, because I knew somehow, I felt inside that something was gonna happen. I talked to this lady and she was saying where are you at, and are you OK, and why are you crying and she was real concerned, and I said I can't do it anymore, I can't take care of my little boy, I need some help, and this lady says please just sit down for a while, take a deep breath and relax 'cause you need to stop crying here [...] I sat down and I was just talking to her and releasing all this, you know, I need a friend to talk to. So then I hung with her and she told me to call her again if I was feeling like this again. Then I was looking through the phone book, [...] I was just look for anything to dial and I came across this, and it said it was some childcare center, [...] I called but I just hung up again. I didn't want to hurt my kid but I did.

In the requests for help, the importance of being a good mother came through (Hewitson, 2000). Stanton et al. (2000) intensively studied seven cases of maternal infanticide and find that "being a good mother was important to all the women" (p. 1454) and they were "attempting to be the best mother possible" (Hewitson, 2000, p. 2).

Lacking alternatives to remedy their social isolation and inability to escape, medical services are often all some mothers have for help escaping the stressful situation (Wade et al., 2005). Crying is the one of the primary reasons parents seek health care for their infant child (Barr, 1990; Gottesman, 2007). For mothers and children in poverty, the economic resources needed to gain medical attention are not always readily available and seeking help with a crying baby from the medical community may not be an option. This leaves the mother trapped and perceiving herself as having no alternative but to gain compliance from the infant. This requires perseverance, but often also includes increasing use of force.

5.6.   Using Force to Gain Compliance

With this background as life history, the stage is set for the situational precipitating events of stress, powerlessness, failure, and an inability to escape commonly reports in cases of infanticide (Alder & Baker, 1997; Cummins & Mueller, 1994; Jensen, 2001; Oberman & Meyer, 2001, 2008; Smithey, 1997, 1998). Female-perpetrated infanticide occurs under conditions or in the context of intense conflict and when the mother perceives no other solution to her desperate situation (Smithey, 1998, 2001). Such desperation and powerlessness are born from a lack of economic resources, an inability to escape, and a perceived lack of other options due to the institutionalization of expectations of mothers (Alder & Baker, 1997; Giddens, 1979, 1984).

Unable to gain compliance, the mothers studied increased force as they continued their attempts to stop the baby's crying. The force has the goal of "reaffirming face" (Goffman, 1967) by standing her ground as a capable mother. To act otherwise would be to confirm questions of face and self as a capable mother perceived as being raised by the victim's noncompliant, continued crying. At this stage the choice was to continue force or increase its use in an attempt to gain compliance.

> He was fine that morning, he had got up about six something and we went to take care of some stuff (run errands) and the baby had used it (urinated) on himself. Then, I made him sit in the corner. Later he used it again then I whupped him. Nothing stopped him. Whuppings, sittin' in the corner, he didn't care.

> We (subject and her boyfriend) was having trouble potty training him. We made him sit on the potty for an hour. Then he (boyfriend) beat him. I made him sit on the potty some more, then I whipped him good.

> I couldn't get her to eat so I put her in her room for a while. She cried and I thought now maybe she'll eat. She kept crying and wouldn't eat. I put her on the floor and left the room. I could still hear her crying. I went back in the living room and hit her and told her she had to eat. She still wouldn't eat.

The social expectations of the mothering ideology that define good mothering as being capable of assuaging crying babies, potty training, and eating on schedule has rendered these mothers powerless in the face of a crying baby (Alder & Baker, 1997). The subsequent perceived lack of options creates an immediate, daily-life environment that constrains their choices and decisions (Sommers & Baskin, 1993). In times of intense suffering and powerlessness, the self begins to focus not on itself as an agent, but increasingly on the pain that it feels. The breakdown in tolerance and the management of ideas, beliefs, arouse anger, frustration, and fear that exponentially magnify the source of the failure. Social support is unavailable and coping mechanisms – which can be sheer will for those in absolute poverty – (Ogle et al., 1996) break down. The feelings "consume the negativity" and come to reflect hatred of the baby (Barr & Beck, 2008). An assault is imminent.

5.7. The Assault

5.7.1. *Stage V: Fatal Injury by the Mother*

The assault is born from the mother's pain caused by increasingly reduced options and rationality which takes her to a point of no longer being able to conceive of options. Potentially, there are two categories of mothers who lethally assault their infants – those who are in such an emotional state that they become incapable of cognitively processing the consequences of their actions and those that retain this capacity but are lashing back at the situational context of entrapment and unmet expectations. As a mother in Barr and Beck's (2008) study stated, "you are so angry it's like a rage, it's all-consuming [...] and you can't stop it" (p. 1717.e3). The rage is acute mental incapacitation and anger at the powerlessness and hopelessness that emerges in the context of the cultural inequity and contradictions represented by the crying baby (Alder & Baker, 1997; Giddens, 1979, 1984; Hays, 1996; Smithey, 2001). As Stroud (2008) concludes, "those who [...] used extreme violence demonstrated a lack of empathy, perceiving the victim as provoking or deserving the attack" (p. 493). Given the inordinate amount of care required for infants and the often accompanying chronic sleep deprivation, minor demands by the infant are experienced as intense stressors heavy-laden with resentment. The inability to escape the chronically stressful social context makes the mere presence of the infant provocative (Stanton et al., 2000). This context fits the interpersonal state of the mother that is often referred to as "losing it." Mothers describe this state as screaming and hitting while in an irrational state of expecting the baby to comply with her demands.

Jensen (2001) finds corroborative evidence that women resort to adult homicide as a result of suffering due to chronic situational stresses that act as triggers. Additionally, the predisposing factors discussed in Chapter 2 result in broken down coping mechanisms and anger management skills, which are already low among those with "damaged selves" (Crimmins et al., 1997). The result is overwhelming anger from the inability to escape the challenge, a sense of complete failure, and the unwantedness of the entire situation. The rage is apparent in the descriptions these mother gave of how they fatally injured their infants.

> I did it. I don't blame anyone but myself. I was feeding him and he urinated on me. I jumped up and he fell to the floor. Then I picked him up, shook him, and banged his head on something in the living room (the police report states it was a coffee table).

> I hit her in the head with a stick, and a belt, I hit her with my fist on the head, then I threw her on the floor.

Rage does not have to be a physical catharsis that involves multiple blows and injuries. Rage can be a single, physical overpowering of the victim that is sustained long enough to produce death.

> I was so tired of his crying that I put my hand over his mouth
> and kept it there until I was sure he had stopped.

The power of gender socialization of the unrealistic expectations that form the mother identity rendered the mothers "blind" or unable to recognize or consider options. The power of social institutions does not allow her to be innovative and requires that she stay with the suffering, stressful context until she succeeds. Walking away before she injures the child requires rational thought or the cognitive ability to convince herself to leave despite the constraint that it must be the mother who achieves the expectations of a happy baby. She is in an emotional state and thinking about physically removing herself requires a level of rationality that is rare once a mother has been challenged and reaches a point where the infant's actions are personalized. It requires also that she act in defiance of social sanctions. The infant becomes the target of her rage or agency to eliminate or resolve the unwanted situation. She is powerless and she cannot escape.

Chapter 6

Primary Prevention and Social Change

The cases and research findings presented in this book are at the extreme end of violence toward children. While a continuum may be a useful tool, we should not assume that the lethal injury of an infant is any less violent than an assault on a toddler or older child. This makes difficult a continuum of violence from minor to lethal injury as physiological vulnerability of the infant interacts with age. Put bluntly, a two-year old can withstand the same level of lethal violence for a two-month old and will probably survive the assault. This results in a more dangerous context for very young infants. As discussed in Chapter 1, other than neonates, infants up to four months of age are at greatest risk, in part due to physiological vulnerability. As a society we cannot do anything about expediting the growth of an infant, but we can do something about the social conditions under which they grow.

The suggestions for change addressed in this chapter are applicable to all levels of violence toward children of any age but are born from my research on lethal injury of children under 32 months of age. I discuss needed social change and possible, short-term interventions of stressors, many of which are common to all mothers. Changing them not only reduces the possible conflux of all or most of the stressors that generate the pivotal point of "losing it" but would also increase the quality of life for mothers and children in general.

I offer two theoretical premises in this book: (1) the current mothering ideology is unrealistic, anomic, and impossible for one person to fulfill and (2) mothers are not allowed to escape the chronic suffering from raising a baby, often unwanted, without sufficient resources. Based on these premises, I offer suggestions for primary prevention and restructuring secondary prevention.

6.1. Primary Prevention

Primary prevention consists of actions designed to lower the incidence of a social problem by counteracting harmful circumstances before they have a chance to produce violence (Smithey & Straus, 2003). This form of prevention is more socially pervasive and effective than secondary treatment and has the greatest potential for reducing violence against children. Stop romanticizing and teach the reality of child rearing, support for family planning, continued education and social nonacceptance of hitting children, change the expectations or give families more time and resources to meet them, economic equality for women, and providing more meaningful support are preventive measures that will improve the social conditions under which we raise our children.

6.1.1.   Stop Romanticizing and Teach the Reality of Child Rearing

While no one can be completely prepared for the reality of the time consumption, intensive labor, lack of sleep, almost constant cajoling the infant into better humor, and the relentless, stressful task of figuring out what a crying baby needs, we should strive to better prepare everyone, including males. The reality of mothering catches most mothers off-guard even when it is not their first child. First-born children carry the greatest potential for unpreparedness but each child is different and the time, emotion, and costs of an additional child can be exponentially stressful. The mothers researched were not prepared and, once in the throes of mothering, felt compelled to mask (Maushart, 1999) it to avoid harsh judgment. Requiring mothers to mask hides the reality of parenting from others and is another stressor in the already complex environment of mothering.

An important part of preparing people for parenting is teaching them there is not a "one size fits all" method, that every child is different, and that they are going to be frequently lost as to what to do and struggling with an unhappy baby that cannot communicate its needs. The belief of maternal instinct should be less rigid to allow mothers to realize that they will not always have positive feelings toward their children and that expressing their feelings to others is a sign of strength. Finally, we should emphasize that mothering is struggle and an inability to assuage a crying baby is not a significant symbol of failing the mothering identity.

6.1.2.   Support for Family Planning

The earliest primary prevention is avoiding mistimed or unwanted pregnancies. The emotion work of being a mother begins before the conception of the fetus. While arguably unrealistic or naively done, the ability to meet the expectations of mothering begins well before the reality of mothering is realized. This investment and emotional desire may be an intervening variable between the infliction of a lethal injury and "catching oneself." We need better policy to reduce unwanted children and families should have a higher priority (Barber et al., 1999). Contraception and safe, nonstigmatizing abortions in supportive environments should be more affordable and available to avoid unwanted or mistimed pregnancies.

6.1.3.   Social Nonacceptance of Hitting Children

The social mandate of corporal punishment and the teaching of hitting as a means of controlling the child should not be part of the mothering ideology expectations of well-behaved children. Child homicide cases are not significantly different from most cases of harsh punishment or child abuse that started as a "spanking" (Adinkrah, 2001; Crittenden & Craig, 1990; Mugavin, 2005) and are described as "rehearsals" for the lethal assault (Smithey, 1998, 2001). Corporal punishment has been found to set the stage for nonlethal assault (American Academy of Pediatrics, 1998; Gershoff, 2008; Straus, 2001). Laws that prohibit corporal punishment have been passed in some states but this has not been supported by society as a whole, partly because the lengthy history of spanking has left parents with little else for knowing how to manage children. Our society emphasizes this method more than others and provides very little time and opportunity to use other techniques of parenting. Spanking is a quick and easy response. It is much less time and attention consuming than other parenting techniques and has a long history of mistaken religious belief in sparing the rod spoils the child (Straus, 2001). This mandate is founded in the unrealistic expectation that children should always be well-behaved and that parents should be able to control their children at all times. "Well-behaved" is typically operationalized as quiet, overly polite, and immediately responsive to adult commands. Yet at the same time, we recognize the lack of cognitive and social development of children. At some point, these contradictory realities make one or the other infeasible. Learning these behaviors is important for succeeding in life but the immediacy at which we expect them to be learned is unrealistic and often stems from parents not having the time or emotional energy needed to expect a less urgent response from the child.

6.1.4. Change the Expectations of Mothering …

To a large extent, my call for changing the mothering ideology is an intangible request for individuals to rethink their beliefs about good mothering and to recognize that mothering behavior they may witness has a very complex background. Part of the mask of good mothering is to appear happy, loving, and in control. (Maushart, 1999). Unfortunately, masking also hides the strain and complexities of raising children. Consequently, many people do not see the reality of parenting but assume they would do things better if they were attending to that child at that moment. This major, often unfounded assumption upholds the cultural and economic inequality of mothers.

More importantly, we need to stop assuming that mothers who are struggling to manage the child-rearing context and fulfill the ideology are inherently "bad" mothers. Mother-bashing is a way of socially controlling mothers toward the mothering ideology and its requirement that "good" mothering is successful only if her baby is happy, healthy, and well-behaved. Harshly judging or condemning mothers when they are angry, visibly frustrated, or chronically struggling to manage a child only escalates her negative emotions (Bernard, 1990). Helping mothers de-escalate and manage time, if not also gain resources, allows for stress reduction in the forms of a break and reduced worry over needed goods, shows care and support to a mother who may need positive, social validation. A positive, support response to a struggling mother also conveys a recognition of the enormous task she is attempting to fulfill, and creates space for possible, positive mother–child interaction, immediately if not long term. Mothers need to find reward and positive circumstances wherever they can to restore or recharge their energy. Experiencing someone responding positively to both herself and her crying baby may improve her esteem, or at least not challenge it, and lead her to no longer see the baby as a crying, impossible object but as a valuable human, albeit through someone else's eyes. At a minimum, it could make her refocus and reflect. Offering a sympathetic smile instead of stares and glares sends the message that you recognize how difficult it is to raise a child.

Negatively responding to mothers results in self-isolation as a means to avoid judgment and mother-bashing that produce an overall sense of failing. Such labeling increases her self-isolation. The shaming and humiliation does little toward moving her toward rationality and does plenty in moving her toward "losing it." In this way, mother-bashing increases the chances of anger and violence toward children.

Changing the expectations also means addressing the disorganization and contradictions of the mothering ideology content that have exponentially grown and become more emotionally and labor-intensive (see Hays, 1996; Hochschild, 1997). Due to the anomic state of the ideology, mothers are often clueless, insecure, and confused about what they should do and why (Bernard, 1975; Maushart, 1999). We need to rewrite our public discourse (Rossiter, 1988) on the subject of motherhood that tells us simultaneously "everything" and "nothing" that we need to know (Maushart, 1999). At a minimum, we should change the perceptions and conversation from "bad mothers" to "bad environments" in which the children are being raised. Focusing on the stressful, entrapping environments where mothers struggle to meet the demands of a child and fear scrutiny clarifies the causes as social and not always individual. Anytime we blame individuals for a social problem without accounting for the social conditions that are common to those individuals, we alleviate society from any responsibility for solving the problem.

Reducing the sheer volume of unrealistic expectations of mothers would go a long way toward alleviate the confusing, strainful context many women abide for decades as they raise children and would increase the overall quality of life for both women and children. Reducing and organizing the expectations would ease much of the strain experienced by mothers and reduce the intellectual demands to triage information or, as Hays (1996) describes it "sort the mail." This is an enormous task that should begin by regulating the child-rearing informational industry. Stopping the flood of scientifically untested "how-to-parent" information from the child-rearing industry will reduce the amount of often-contradictory expectations. The industry should be held accountable by requiring that child-rearing advice have scientific support, much like the social work, psychology, and medical fields. Without systematic scrutiny, it is a capitalistic enterprise that has lost sight of its original purpose – to help mothers effectively manage child development. Reducing the daily increase of new information on how to parent would streamline the goals, values, and techniques of parenting into more manageable practices.

Finally, we need to change the ideology of mothering by widening the work of childcare to more than just the mother. Our belief that it has to be the mother and that she is naturally compelled to care for her children upholds this criterion and the suffering of mothers as the only ones who must endure this enormous task. Instead of intensifying mother as we have done over the past few decades (Hays, 1996), we need to lessen it.

6.1.5. ... or Give Families More Time and Resources to Meet the Expectations

If we are unwilling to reduce and socially organize the expectations of "good" mothering, then we should provide families the resources and time necessary to fulfill them. This provision should include economic equality for women and providing meaningful social support to families, including restructuring social services with greater economic support and disconnecting them from the some of power of the civil and criminal justice system.

Women's economic status is a universal finding in infant homicide studies (Hunnicutt & LaFree, 2008). Addressing the economic stressors that contribute to infanticide is important because the largest group of poor people in the US is women and their children (U. S. Census Bureau, 2015). A recent study by the Institute for Women's Policy Research (Hegewisch & Williams-Baron, 2017) reports that women are almost half of the workforce. They are the sole or co-breadwinner in half of American families with children and receive more college and graduate degrees than men. Despite their breadwinner status and educational attainment, women continue to earn considerably less than men on average. In 2016, female full-time, year-round workers made only 80.5 cents for every dollar earned by men, a gender wage gap of 20%. The authors conclude that there is no other plausible explanation for the robust trends of economic inequality than cultural beliefs regarding women's structured reduction in pay and advancement. Economic equality would reduce the number of families "stretching" the already unequal paycheck of women and diminish the stress mothers in the poverty, working, and middle classes manage daily. In addition to equal pay, discrimination and all forms of mommy tracking must stop. Changes in workplace, attitudes, and power differentials that allow discrimination against mothers should be proactively addressed at the management and interpersonal levels. Structuring a supportive work environment that balances time for mothers and fathers to attend to their families would decrease cultural inequality also as fathers would be allowed more time for care of their children.

6.1.6. An Ability to Escape

Maternal infanticide is in response to being trapped in a chronically stressful environment. An escape or periodic breaks from mothering would make a difference in the likelihood of violence against children. Hays (1996) concludes that the quality of the time [mothers] spend with their kids actually seems to increase when they have a chance to be away from them for part of the day. "A break ... reinforces your feeling of competence and therefore results in more rewarding time with your children" (p. 148).

Equality at home would create more breaks from childcare. While there may be recent gains in reducing this inequality, there is still a significant imbalance in time devoted and the nature of the household tasks performed by men. Men have more ability to schedule leisure time due to the episodic nature of the house work they do and leisure time for mothers is much less than for fathers and other adults (Hochschild, 1989, 1997; Mattingly & Bianchi, 2003; Milkie, Mattingly, Nomagrechi, Bianchi, & Robinson, 2004). As concluded by Bianchi (2000), "gender segregation of tasks continues, with wives performing the "core, traditional feminine tasks to a larger degree and men concentrating their household labor on other, more episodic or discretionary tasks" (p. 209).

Sherman (2017) finds that women strongly prefer equal sharing with regard to housework, childcare, and income generation, with no desire for either partner to be a primary breadwinner. Men prefer a more gendered division of responsibility in which they are the breadwinners with less housework and childcare responsibilities. This preference underscores how this inequality is due to tradition and cultural belief.

Even under circumstances where fathers contribute to house care and childcare more than other fathers, new mothers lose their ability to create a zone of privacy or separateness (Ogle et al., 1996) from infant care. Developing other socially acceptable options for mothers to step-back and having a moment to reflect on their stressful context would reduce violence toward children. Such options could include proactive reaching out by friends and family but must be done so in a nonjudgmental way. Having family and friends available for support reduces the likelihood of violence against the infant in three ways. First, the ability to reach out to another adult potentially allows emotional support and collaborative, reflective intelligence, depending on the response of the other adult. Second, the presence of another adult in the stressful context can serve as guardianship over the infant. Third, another adult may create an ability to physically escape, even if temporarily, when the other person takes over the immediate task of childcare.

However, the reliance on extended family support is structurally limited by the lack of time and resources they have to share often making this option tentative. Extended families are overwhelmed and under-resourced too. The majority of families in our society live less than paycheck-to-paycheck (Department of Labor, 2016) which may be better described as living week-to-week. Paychecks are often spent before they are received. And, if not, they are spent within one to two days of receipt. Families without wage-paying jobs, live day-to-day. Families are caught in a cycle from which they cannot escape. Regardless of how much they may wish to help the new mothers and babies in their families, they may not able because their own economic resources and time are consumed by financial "survival." Many valiant attempts at trying to incorporate the expenses of a newborn into their larger family obligations fail within a matter of weeks or months. For some, resentment may build as they realize the small amount of economic and time relief from which they suffered as they had finished raising their own children is short-lived.

To expect extended family to be able to take care of the mother and her new born, and possibly other children, is tantamount to expecting a single mother with no resources to raise a newborn. Still, the vast majority of extended family members and friends try, even if for a short time. It is the commitment of families in our society that keep this institution intact. The social institutions of economics and government do much less comparatively. We need our families to commit and support each other as a unit, both emotionally and economically. But we also need an equal commitment from society both economically with better wages, shorter workdays, health care, and housing and emotionally by allowing more time for parenting, marriage, and family activities.

Because family and personal support are tentative and unpredictable, affordable daycare is a much-needed form of support and relief (Bernard, 1975; Wade et al., 2005). Its consistency and predictability provide the anticipation of breaks that mothers can focus on as a source of perseverance during long, challenging intervals of childcare.

Another contributor to child violence is social isolation. It is the result of the inability to escape and the need to avoiding exposing one's bad mothering or failed attempts. It is the fear of judgment that isolates her. The judgment can regard being a "bad mother," being a victim of intimate partner violence, or both.

Social service support groups and organizing nearby mother support groups should provide options for urgent situations but must be done so without fear of repercussions. Most people turn to informal support out of familiarity, some degree of security, and out of a fear of formal support. Informal networks can reach out. If each person "adopts" a mother–child situation in their life, such as a sibling, friend, or neighbor with a baby, and offer occasional support, not only would that increase the mother's ability to escape, it would serve also to make visible and spread the reality of parenting. But first, we have to make it acceptable to ask for help.

In a capitalist, competitive society, asking for help or admitting that one is struggling is viewed as a sign of weakness. This view contributes to our cultural belief that good mothers are not weak. There needs to be a shift in public attitudes toward eliminating harsh judgment of help seeking by mothers. Mothers should be able to ask directly for help without fear of negative judgment and consequences. Again, belief in maternal instinct and automatic maternal attachment makes it difficult for mothers to ask for help (Kline, 1995) by framing the request as "unnatural" and the mother as biologically inferior and not fit to be a parent (Hewitson, 2000).

One seemingly legitimate avenue for seeking help is getting medical attention and often is all mothers have for help escaping the stressful situation (Wade et al., 2005). This strategy is an indirect manner of asking for help and even then the mother usually does not divulge the full details of her stressful situation. Still, for the few details she may give, the medical setting has the potential advantage of her avoiding mother-bashing. Illness of a child is viewed as outside of the mother's control and alleviates her from the responsibility to make the baby stop crying. By seeking medical help, the mother is creating a break from the overwhelming expectations of being a "good mother" and temporarily passing the burden to others. It may be that the infant is in fact ill or that medication for a few days will reduce its intensive care at home. Either way, the medical arena is a prime place for integration with social services.

6.1.7. Restructure Secondary Prevention to Provide More Meaningful Social Support to Families

We are aware that on some level, social and government support fall way short of economically and emotionally helping mothers (Gauthier, Chaudoir, & Forsyth, 2003). Families in our society are overwhelmed, have low priority in the allocation of wealth and social goods, and are undervalued as an important social institution. Providing more structured support for families means providing more support for agencies that deal with families. Social service workers should be available to work with all degrees of family problems, not just serious ones. For families to receive resources, including the amount of time and attention paid to the case, *after* serious abuse has happened is counterproductive to society and the well-being of families. Any call about concern for a family should be met with some degree of nonpunitive attention. Social service agents should be available for emotional support without repercussions that are tantamount to policing families, not protecting children (Besharov, 1998). Otherwise we are not preventing abuse but only responding to families after the problems escalate into seriousness.

We need to provide mental health care that is more holistic regarding a mother's life and not just focused on a single event or behavior. It must address her immediate social environment and include her support system and others who are co-producers of the unhealthy environment, such as violent intimate partners. Stanton et al. (2000) identified a "circular process whereby denial of the seriousness of previous abuse [...] by members of the support networks fed back to augment each other and undermine the urgency with which the cases might have otherwise been viewed" (p. 1452).

The problem with families and friends denying and minimizing the abuse is the belief there will not be an immediate, supportive, and effective response by social services, the medical community, or the criminal justice system. Family members are very aware of the rapid loss of control over decisions regarding care. This is not the objective of their actions nor are they always able to care for the child or children if the mother is jailed or hospitalized. The factors considered (and ignored) regarding intervention efforts toward violent family members are shaped by the family's own powerlessness, helplessness, and lack of resources, especially poor and minority women. Formal intervention should be coproduced with input and recommendations from family members who retain some degree of control over their loved one's circumstances.

Often the decisions made by social service and healthcare professions are done with insufficient time given to the case and with heavy reliance on intake procedures that are not individually customized. Secondary prevention is necessary and important but its implementation is often problematic, most notably the strong desire for risk assessment factors (Besharov, 1998) and the criminalization of "poor" parenting. This type of prevention requires social service agents to identify the likely circumstances and characteristics of potential abusers and the line or set of risk factors that, when crossed, result in violence. However, given the complexities of social circumstances and the wide variation in individual capabilities, interpretations, and life experiences, there cannot be a constant or "one size fits all" approach to identification. As we learned from the attempts during the 1970s and 1980s to identify the risk factors of child abuse and traits of women likely to become victims of intimate partner violence (Gelles, 1978; Gelles & Straus, 1988), as the studies accumulated, more factors were added to the risk profile. As this happens, the potential for identifying a future offender is greatly reduced as the profile increasingly includes more and more persons. In other words, as we identify more and more risk factors, we widen the net to the point that an increasingly large number of persons fall within the parameters of "risk." Not only does this make risk profiling ineffective, it also increases the likelihood of "false positives" or labeling someone as a potential offender. This type of labeling can lead to the very behavior or type of person it attempts to prevent (Lemert, 1951). By labeling a mother a "poor" mother, she becomes more closely scrutinized by social services, possibly the criminal justice system, and family and friends who become aware of the structured surveillance activities, such as home visits or meetings with children's services. This increases her stress rather than reducing it.

Unfortunately, social science and formal agents or practitioners want an answer that does not seem to exist and repeatedly expect and try to produce "risk" factors that have preventive power. The need for measurable markers of impending harmful behavior is due to expediency as social services workers are heavily overworked and under-resourced. The time needed to become intensively familiar with a family is not given to the workers. Instead they are taught to "score" families and follow a prescribed range of sanctions.

We cannot eliminate practices of social services because there are children in need of protection. What we can do is change the practices and response by social services once a mother is identified as "at risk." Government entities, family, and friends must become less condemning of mothers in need of help in order to reduce her stress at home and increase the chances of her asking for help and fully disclosing, rather than concealing her situation. As it stands now, mothers fear social services scrutiny, do not often ask for help, and when she does ask, the few resources our society has to help come too late. There is a "canceling effect" between the efforts social services and medical professionals make to identify mother at risk and the use of risk factors that is seriously undermined by subsequent criminal justice, civil courts, and other forms of social control that take a punitive and controlling stance toward struggling mothers. A greater devotion of resources to helping families would reduce the need for risk factors. Until we do this, social services workers will have little choice but to continue using expedient assessment tools.

Criminalization may have served the purpose of transforming violence against children from an individual to a social problem, but punishing mothers and families only compounds the problem. The currently harsh societal and criminal justice system response results in greater fear of being a bad mom, decreased likelihood of asking for help, and lessened power of mothers. The economically poor especially are fearful of turning to or relying on formal support due to the criminalization of "bad" mothering. The fear is not unfounded as court personnel are not understanding of the economic (Kline, 1995) and cultural stress experienced by mothers, especially poverty-class mothers.

The improving of social services and its accessibility to all families must be accompanied by a simultaneous decrease in the severity of societal response by decriminalizing "bad" mothering. This requires bringing social services out from under the power of the criminal and civil courts. A system where many cases can be handled outside the purview of the courts would reduce the fear social service workers themselves experience from contempt of court rulings against them. There should be more constraint on judges threatening and using this charge. A number of such charges occur because social service workers have conflicting time obligations to either be available in the courtroom when the case is heard, which may be hours or days of waiting at the courthouse, or to do the work required by the court before the next hearing. Either way, the issue, again, is more economic support for a larger work force of social service workers who have realistic caseloads and time to improve practices. For example, a frequently used means of social services and the courts for managing cases of struggling mothers and families is sending one or both parents to parenting classes. These classes need to be more than "meet-n-teach" and the curriculum should be based on scientifically tested child development techniques and integrated into a more comprehensive, support package that includes home-based learning. Mothers receiving more frequent positive, supportive home visits have a significant reduction in stress and conflicts and viewed their children more positively, and have improved well-being (Nations, 2005). The structure of the classes should be dynamic to make sure that when a mother gives up her limited time to go to a class, even if against her will, that is small, dynamic, and interactive. This requires more time and attention given to cases.

There are numerous other suggestions for primary prevention and restructuring secondary treatment that raise hard questions that we, as a society, must ask ourselves. To what extent should we change this unrealistic, anomic belief system that clearly oppresses women? Contemporary mothering is rapidly becoming even more labor-intensive, emotionally draining, and requires enormous sacrifice – both personally and economically (Hays, 1996). Are we damaging our mothers by continually reproducing economic and cultural inequality? And, as my work and that by others finds, are we not in fact putting our children at great risk for injury and possibly death? To what extent are we, as a society, in need of proactive social change to reclaim, empower, and reform mothering and the entire family social institution?

APPENDIX A

Intensive Interview Guide

Date(s):

Description of location (e.g., correctional facility, parole office, private location, etc.):

Time(s):

Code#:

Pseudonym:

Age:

Residence Pattern:

born in_____ (large city, medium city, village, rural) lived there until _____
(repeat for each residence)

Special comment on residence pattern:

Birth Order: 1st____ 2nd____ 3rd____ 4th____ 5th____ 6th____ Other:____

No. of Brothers: _____ Ages relative to subject: _____

No. of Sisters: _____ Ages relative to subject: _____

Parents: Biological Mother: ____ Age at Subject's birth_____

Currently living: Yes _____   No _____

$\downarrow$

Year died_____

Subject's Age _____

Cause of Death _____

Biological Father: Age at Subject's birth _____
Currently living: Yes _____   No _____

$\downarrow$

Year died_____

Subject's Age _____

Cause of Death _____

Parents' Marital Status:
Never Married _____ Married _____ Divorced _____

↓

Subject's age _____
Year(s) Mother Remarried

_____

Year(s) Father Remarried

_____

Ages lived with Mother

_____

Ages lived with Father

_____

Family/Childhood History:

History of Family Structure/Living Arrangements (i.e., Blended, Family, Foster Care, Adoption, Children's Home, etc.)

From your birth to your first marriage/cohabitation, describe the different houses you have lived in and whether or not you lived there with your family.

Parenting Practices of Parents/Guardian:

> When you were growing up, were there any rules or schedules you had to follow? Please describe them.
>
> What happened when you broke a rule or did not follow the schedule?
>
> What would your mother do? How angry would she get?
>
> What would your father do? How angry would he get?

Emotional Openness and Support:

> When you had a problem or something was bothering you who would you most likely talk to, your mother or your father? (Ask for explanation.)

Relationship with Siblings:

> How many brothers/sisters do you have?
>
> How well did you get along with them?

Current Relationships with Family Members:

> Do you ever talk to, write or see your parents/guardians?
>
> How would you describe your relationship with them now?
>
> Do you ever talk to, write or see any of your siblings?
>
> How would you describe your relationship with them now?

Education:

Highest Level _____ Year Attained _____

Special Comments: (dropout, vocational training)

Employment Record:

1) Job Description:
   Dates: Salary:
   Level of Satisfaction:
   (Repeat for each job)

Marital Status: Never Married _____ Married _____
                                                    ↓
    Year Married _____ Divorced _____ Race of spouse _____
    Year Married _____ Divorced _____ Race of spouse _____
Cohabitation (i.e., lived for a while with a man who is not your husband):
    Never Cohabited _____ Cohabited _____
                                                    ↓
    from _____to _____ Race/ethnicity of partner _____
    from _____to _____ Race/ethnicity of partner _____

Other Significant Relationships:
Have there been any other relationships during which you would stay at his house for several days at a time or he would stay at yours? Please describe them.

Children:
Date Of Birth _____ Gender _____ Race/ethnicity _____
Which Marriage/Cohabitation/Boyfriend _____

Is this child now living?   Yes_____   No _____
                                                    ↓
    Age at Death _____ Year Died _____
    Cause of Death _____

    (Repeat for each child):

Expectations of Marriage:

Expectations held by subject:
    Describe a good wife. Where do you think you learned this?
    Is this different from what other people think?
    Do you think you are/were a good wife to any or all of your spouses/partners? Why or why not?
    Describe a good husband. Where do you think you learned this?
    Is this different from what other people think?
    Do you think your husband/partner is/was a good husband/partner?

Expectations of Parenting:

Expectations held by subject:
    Describe the ideal family. If you could create the perfect family, what would it look like? What would it do? How would it act?
    What did you think raising a child would be like? Did you have specific goals or dreams?
    Describe a "good mother". Where do you think you learned this?
    Do you think you are/were a good mother? What did you do, think, or say that makes you think you are/were (are not/were not) a good mother.

Do you think your mother is/was a good mother? What did she do, think, or say that makes you think she is/was (is not/was not) a good mother.

As a mother yourself, how much did you want to be like your mother? (ask for elaboration).

Describe a "good father". Where do you think you learned this?

Do you think your father is/was a good father? What did he do, think, or say that makes you think he is/was (are not/was not) a good father.

Do you think the baby's father is/was a good father? What did he do, think, or say that makes you think he is/was (are not/was not) a good father.

How much did you want the baby's father to be like your father? (ask for elaboration).

If you could go back, as far back as you want, what would you change or have turn out differently?

Expectations held by baby's father:

Did the baby's father ever talk about his childhood and family? What did he say?

Did the baby's father ever talk about his idea of the perfect family? What did he say?

What did the baby's father think raising a child would be like? Did he have specific goals or dreams?

Conception of the Deceased Infant:

Describe your relationship with the biological father:

How did you meet?

How long had you known each other?

Were you living together? If so, for how long?

How well did you get along?

Were you comfortable discussing problems in your relationship?

Who made the decisions?

The Pregnancy:

Gestation term: Was the baby full-term?

Did you have any physical difficulties while you were pregnant?

How many weeks pregnant were you when you realized you were pregnant?

How did you feel about having a baby?

Was abortion considered? If yes,

Who did you discuss this with?

What steps were taken toward getting an abortion (e.g., get information about abortions, locate nearest clinic, determine cost, etc.)?

Family Support:

Baby's Father:

How many weeks pregnant were you when you told him you were pregnant?

How did he feel about you having a baby?

Do you think he would have approved of an abortion?

Did he ever mention abortion as a possible alternative to the pregnancy?

Did he ever discuss what the future would be like with a baby? What did he say?

Subject's Mother:

How many weeks pregnant were you when you told her you were pregnant?

How did she feel about your having a baby?

Was she helpful? If so, how?

Do you think she would have approved of an abortion?

Did she ever mention abortion as a possible alternative to the pregnancy?

Subject's Father:

How many weeks pregnant were you when you told him you were pregnant?

How did he feel about your having a baby?

Was he helpful?

Do you think he would have approved of an abortion?

Did he ever mention abortion as a possible alternative to the pregnancy?

Subject's Children (if relevant):

How old were each of your children during the pregnancy?

How did they feel about having a new brother or sister?

Subject's Relatives:

Did you have any other relatives with whom you maintained regular contact? (For each one listed, ask the following):

Title: _____

How many weeks pregnant were you when you told him/her you were pregnant?

How did s/he respond?

Was s/he helpful?

Do you think s/he would have approved of an abortion?

Did s/he ever mention abortion as a possible alternative to the pregnancy?

Prenatal Care:

Frequency of Doctor Visits:

Rest, Diet, and General State of Health:

Birth of the Infant:

Weight/Height:

Were there any difficulties during the labor/delivery?

What medication did you use during the labor/delivery?

Length of stay in hospital:

Were there any physical problems following birth?

Did you tell your doctor about these problems? If so, what did the doctor say?

Support from the baby's father:
>   Was the baby's father at the hospital or home during the labor and delivery?
>   What did he do during this time?

Support from subject's mother:
>   Was your mother at the hospital or home during the labor and delivery?
>   What did she do during this time?

Support from subject's father:
>   Was your father present at the hospital or home during the labor and delivery?
>   What did he do?

Support from Others:
>   Name any other persons who were helpful during the pregnancy and describe the help they gave.

Economic Situation
>   Did you have a job at this time? If so, what type of job?
>   Did you have any other sources of income? Please describe these resources.
>   Does/did the baby's father provide money or any other resources to you or the baby? Please describe these resources.

Living Environment:
>   Physically describe the house or apartment you were living in at the time of the baby's birth.
>   Who owned the house or apartment?
>   How many children did you have at this time?
>   Were there any others living in the household?
>   Were there any other children living in the household?

Parenting Practices:
Those used by subject:
>   What type of rules or schedules did you have for your children?
>   How well did your children follow them?
>   What happened if the rules or schedule were not followed?
>   Those used by the "father" of the household:
>   What type of rules or schedules did he have for the children?
>   Did the children follow them?
>   What happened if the rules or schedule were not followed?

Those used by other guardians of the children including the baby's father:
>   What type of rules or schedules did you have for your children?
>   How well did your children follow them?
>   What happened if the rules or schedule were not followed?
>   Those used by the "father" of the household:
>   What type of rules or schedules did he have for the children?
>   Did the children follow them?
>   What happened if the rules or schedule were not followed?

Childcare resources:

Daycare:

> Did you ever use daycare?
>
> When? For how long?
>
> How did you feel about it?
>
> Would you say your life was less or more stressful or about the same when you were using daycare? (ask for elaboration)
>
> Did you continue or discontinue to use daycare? (ask for elaboration)

Family:

> Did your family or your husband/partner's family help with childcare?
>
> How did they help?
>
> How did it make you feel?
>
> Would you say your life was less or more stressful or about the same when you were using daycare? (ask for elaboration)
>
> Did you continue or discontinue to ask your family or the baby's father's family to babysit? (ask for elaboration)

Social Services:

> Did you use any other child resources such as AFDC, Health clinics, etc.? When did you use each of them and for how long?
>
> Did these resources provide help? Relief? Obstacles? Embarrassment?
>
> Would you say your life was less or more stressful or about the same when you were these services? (ask for elaboration)
>
> Which of them did you continue or discontinue to use? (ask for elaboration)

The Death of the Infant:

Starting at any point in time you want, tell me how the baby was injured.

Familial Response:

> Baby's Father's Response:

How did the baby's father respond when he found out about the baby's injuries/death?

> Subject's Mother's Response:

How did your mother respond when she found out about the baby's injuries/death?

> Subject's Father's Response:

How did your father respond when he found out about the baby's injuries/death?

> The Response of Others: How did other friends or relatives respond?

The Funeral:

Who made the arrangements?

Who was present?

How emotionally difficult was it for you? For the baby's father?

History of Mental Illness:

Have you or anyone else ever thought you were mentally ill? If so, please describe what happened.

First Episode:

Age
Diagnosis/Description of Illness
Professional Help: Help sought where?
Medication and hospitalizations
Resolved?   If so, How?
Unresolved?   Currently Active?

(Repeat for each episode):
Other topics/theories/thoughts the subject wishes to talk about:

References

Abel, E. L. (1986). Childhood homicide in Erie County, New York. *Pediatrics*, *77(5)*, 709−713.

Adinkrah, M. (2001). When parents kill: An analysis of filicides in Fiji. *International Journal of Offender Therapy and Comparative Criminology*, *45(2)*, 144−158.

Agnew, R. (1992). Foundation for a general strain theory of crime and delinquency. *Criminology*, *30(1)*, 47−87.

Alder, C., & Baker, J. (1997). Maternal filicide: More than one story to be told. *Women & Criminal Justice*, *9(2)*, 15−39.

American Academy of Pediatrics. (1998). Guidance for effective discipline. *Pediatrics*, *101*(4), 732−728.

American Academy of Pediatrics. (2001). *SIDS and child homicide rulings*. Retrieved from https://www.aap.org/en-us/Pages/Default.aspx

Archer, J. (2000). Sex differences in aggression between heterosexual partners: A meta-analytic review. *Psychological Bulletin*, *126(5)*, 651−680.

Arnot, M. L. (1994). Infant death, child care and the state: The baby-farming scandal and the first infant life protection legislation of 1872. *Continuity and Change*, *9*(2), 271−311.

Ashe, M. (1997). 'Bad mothers' and welfare reform in Massachusetts: The case of Claribel Ventura. In M. Fineman & M. McCluskey (Eds.), *Feminism, media, and the law* (pp. 203−216). New York, NY: Oxford University Press.

Azar, S. T., Miller, E. A., McGuier, D. J., Stevenson, M. T., O'Donnell, E., Olsen, N., & Spence, N. (2016). Maternal social information processing the frequency and severity of mother-perpetrated physical abuse. *Child Maltreatment*, *21*(4), 380−316.

Azar, S. T., Stevenson, M. T., & Johnson, D. R. (2012). Intellectual disabilities and neglectful parenting: Preliminary findings on the role of cognition in parenting risk. *Journal of Mental Health Research in Intellectual Disabilities*, *5*(2), 94−129.

Baca Zinn, M. (1990). Family, feminism, and race in America. *Gender and Society*, *4(1)*, 68−82.

Bandura, A. (1965). Influence of model's reinforcement contingencies of the acquisition of imitative response. *Journal of Personality and Social Psychology*, *1*(6), 589−595.

Bandura, A. (1971). *Social learning theory*. New York, NY: General Learning Press.

Barber, J. S., Axinn, W. G., & Thornton, A. (1999). Unwanted childbearing: Health, and mother-child relationships. *Journal of Health and Social Behavior*, *40(3)*, 231−257.

Baron, L. (1990). Gender inequality and child homicide: A state-level analysis. *Office of Justice Programs, NCJ 136130*. Retrieved from 2017, www.ncjrs.gov/App/Publications/aspx?ID=136130

Barr, J. A., & Beck, C. T. (2008). Infanticide secrets: Qualitative study on postpartum depression. *Canadian Family Physician*, *54*, 1716−1717.e1−5.

Barr, R. G. (1990). The normal crying curve: What do we really know? *Medicine and Child Neurology, 32(4)*, 356–362.

Belknap, J. (1996). *The invisible woman: Gender, crime, and justice*. Belmont, CA: Wadsworth.

Belsky, J., & Kelly, J. (1994). *The transition to parenthood*. New York, NY: Delacorte.

Berger, P. L., & Berger, B. (1972). *Sociology: A biographical approach*. New York, NY: Basic Books.

Berger, P. L., & Luckmann, T. (1966). *The social construction of reality*. Garden City, NY: Doubleday.

Bernard, T. J. (1990). Angry aggression among the truly disadvantaged. *Criminology, 28*(1), 73–95.

Besharov, D. J. (1998). Four commentaries: How we can better protect children from abuse and neglect. *The Future of Children, 8*(1), 120–123.

Bianchi, S. M. (2000). Maternal employment and time with children: Dramatic change or surprising continuity? *Demography, 37*(4), 401–414.

Bianchi, S. M., Robinson, J. P., & Milkie, M. A. (2006). *Changing rhythms of American family life*. New York, NY: Russell Sage Publications.

Blair-Loy, M. (2001). Cultural contradictions of family schemas: The case of women finance executives. *Gender & Society, 15*(5), 687–709.

Bourget, D., & Bradford, J. M. W. (1990). Homicidal parents. *Canadian Journal of Psychiatry, 35*(3), 233–237.

Bourget, D. B., & Gagne, P. (2005). Paternal filicide in Quebec. *Journal of the American Academy of Psychiatry and the Law, 33*(3), 354–360.

Briggs, C. L., & Mantini-Briggs, C. (2000). "Bad mothers" and the threat to civil society: Race, cultural reasoning, and the institutionalization of social inequality in a Venezuelan infanticide trial. *Law and Social Inquiry, 25*(2), 299–354.

Broidy, L., & Agnew, R. (1997). Gender and crime: A general strain theory perspective. *Journal of Research in Crime and Delinquency, 34*(3), 275–306.

Brookman, F., & Nolan, J. (2006). The dark figure of infanticide in England and Wales. *Journal of Interpersonal Violence, 21*(7), 869–889.

Brown, I., & Kennelly, I. (1999). Stereotypes and realities: Black women in the labor market. In I. Brown (Ed.), *Latina and African-American women at work: Race, gender, and economic inequality* (pp. 302–326). New York, NY: Sage.

Budig, M. J., & England, P. (2001). The wage penalty for motherhood. *American Sociological Review, 66*(2), 204–225.

Burgess, R. L., & Akers, R. L. (1968). A differential association-reinforcement theory of criminal behavior. *Social Problems, 14*(2), 128–147.

Catalano, S. M. (2013). *Intimate partner violence: Attributes of victimization, 1993–2011*. Bureau of Justice Statistics Report. Retrieved from https:\\www.bjs.gov/index.cf?mty=pbdetail&iid=4801

Centers for Disease Control CDC. (2012). *Centers for Disease Control*. Washington, DC. Retrieved from https://www.cdc.gov.

Chasnoff, I. J., Hatcher, R., & Burns, W. J. (1982). Polydrug- and methadone-addicted newborns: A continuum of impairment? *Pediatrics, 70*(2), 210–213.

Cherek, D. R., & Steinberg, J. L. (1987). Effects of drugs on human aggressive behavior. *Advances in Human Psychopharmacology, 4*(3), 239–290.

Chew, K. S. Y., McCleary, R., Lew, M. H., & Wang, J. C. (1999). The epidemiology of child homicide in California, 1981 through 1990. *Homicide Studies, 3*(2), 151−169.

Collins, P. H. (1991). *Black feminist thought: Knowledge, consciousness, and the politics of empowerment.* New York, NY: Routledge.

Craig, M. (2004). Perinatal risk factors for neonaticide and infant homicide: Can we identify those at risk? *Journal of the Royal Society of Medicine, 97*(1), 57−61.

Crandall, M., Chiu, B., & Sheehan, K. (2006). Injury in the first year of life: Risk factors and solutions for high-risk families. Paper presented at the First Annual Academic Surgical Congress, San Diego, California. Retrieved from https://academicsurgicalcongress.org/wp-content/uploads/2006/01/ASC14FinalProgram WEB.pdf

Crimmins, S., Langley, S., Brownstein, H. H., & Spunt, B. (1997). Development trends in the nature of child homicide. *Journal of Interpersonal Violence, 5*(2), 202−216.

Crittenden, A. (2001). *The price of motherhood: Why the most important job in the world is still the least valued.* New York, NY: Owl Books.

Crittenden, P. M., & Craig, S. (1990). Developmental trends in child homicide. *Journal of Interpersonal Violence, 5*(2), 202−216.

Cronon, W. (1995). *Uncommon ground: Rethinking the human place in nature.* New York, NY: W. W. Norton.

Cummins, P., & Mueller, B. A. (1994). Infant injury death in Washington State, 1981 through 1990. *Archives of Pediatric and Adolescent Medicine, 148*(10), 1021−1026.

Cutrona, C. E. (1984). Social support and stress in the transition to parenthood. *Journal of Abnormal Psychology, 93*(4), 378−390.

Daniels, R., & Lessow, H. (1964). Severe postpartum reactions. *Psychosomatics, 5*(1), 21−26.

deMause, L. (1988). The evolution of childhood. In L. deMause (Ed.), *Centuries of childhood* (pp. 5−33). New York, NY: Peter Bedrick.

Department of Labor. (2013). *Time use survey.* Washington, DC. Retrieved from https://www.b1s.govtusiatusfaqs.htm.

Department of Labor. (2017). *Time use survey.* Washington, DC. Retrieved from https://www.b1s.govtusiatusfaqs.htm

Dill, B. N. (1994). *Across boundaries of race and class: An exploration of work and family among black female domestic servants.* New York, NY: Garland.

DiMaio, D., & DiMaio, V. J. (2001). *Forensic pathology* (2nd ed.). New York, NY: CRC Press.

d'Orban, P. (1979). Women who kill their children. *British Journal of Psychiatry, 134*(4), 560−571.

Dorne, C. (1989). *Crimes against children.* Chicago, IL: Harrow & Heston.

Dougherty, J. (1993). Women's violence against their children: A feminist perspective. *Women & Criminal Justice, 4*(2), 91−114.

Doyle, D. P., & Luckenbill, D. F. (1991). Mobilizing law in response to collective problems: A test of Black's theory of law. *Law & Society Review, 5*, 103−115.

Durkheim, E. (1895 [1938]). *The rules of sociological method.* S. A. Solovay & J. H. Mueller (Trans.), G. E. G. Caitlin (Ed.). Chicago, IL: The University of Chicago Press.

Durkheim, E. (1897 [1951]). *Suicide: A study in sociology* (G. Simpson, Trans.). New York, NY: Free Press.

Edin, K., & Kefalas, M. (2005). *Promises I can keep: Why poor women put motherhood before marriage.* Berkeley, CA: U. C. Press.

Emery, J. L., & Taylor, E. M. (1986). Investigation of SIDS. *New England Journal of Medicine, 315,* 1675–1676.

Eyer, D. (1993). *Mother-infant bonding: A scientific fiction.* New Haven, CT: Yale University Press.

Falkov, A. (1996). *Study of working together 'Part 8' reports. Fatal child abuse and psychiatric disorder: An analysis of 100 area child protection committee case reviews.* London: Department of Health.

Federal Bureau of Investigation. (2015). *Crime in the United States, 2015.* Retrieved from https://ucr.fbi.gov/crime-in-the-u.s/2015/crime-in-the-u.s.-2015

Ferguson, R. A. (1996). Untold stories in the law. In P. Brooks & P. Gewirtz (Eds.), *Law's stories: Narrative and rhetoric in the law* (pp. 84–98). New Haven, CT: Yale University Press.

Fiala, R., & LaFree, G. (1988). Cross-national determinants of child homicide. *American Sociological Review, 53*(3), 432–445.

Fiske, S. T., & Taylor, S. E. (2013). *Social cognition: From brains to culture.* (2nd ed.). Los Angeles, CA: Sage.

Foucault, M. (1979). *Discipline & punish: The birth of the prison.* New York, NY: Vintage.

Friedman, S. H., Horwitz, S. M., & Resnick, P. J. (2005). Child murder by mothers: A critical analysis of the current state of knowledge and a research agenda. *American Journal of Psychiatry, 162*(9), 1578–1587.

Garfinkel, H. (1965). Conditions of successful degradation ceremonies. *American Journal of Sociology, 61*(5), 420–424.

Gartner, R., & McCarthy, B. (2006). Killing one's children: Maternal infanticide and the dark figure of homicide. In K. Heimer & C. Kruttschnitt (Eds.), *Gender and crime: Patterns in victimization and offending.* New York, NY: NYU Press.

Gauthier, D. A. K., Chaudoir, N. K., & Forsyth, C. J. (2003). A sociological analysis of maternal infanticide in the United States. *Deviant Behavior, 24,* 393–404.

Gelles, R. J. (1978). Etiology of violence: Overcoming fallacious reasoning in understanding family violence and child abuse. Conference proceedings of the Children's Hospital, National Medical Center, Washington, DC.

Gelles, R. J. (1980). Violence in the family: A review of research in the seventies. *Journal of Marriage and the Family, 42*(4), 387–885.

Gelles, R. J. (1991). Physical violence, child abuse, and child homicide: A continuum of violence, or distinct behaviors? *Human Nature, 2*(1), 59–72.

Gelles, R. J., & Straus, M. A. (1988). *Intimate violence.* New York, NY: Simon and Schuster.

Gershoff, E. T. (2008). *Report on physical punishment in the United States: What research tells us about its effect on children.* National Child's Advocacy Center. Retrieved from http://hdl.handle.net/11212/3568

Giddens, A. (1979). *Central problems in social theory: Action, structure, and contradiction in social analysis.* New York, NY: Macmillan.

Giddens, A. (1984). *The constitution of society: Outline of the theory of structuration.* Berkeley, CA: University of California Press.

Goetting, A. (1988). Why parents kill their young children: Detroit 1982–1986. *Journal of Family Violence, 3*(4), 339–346.

Goffman, E. (1959). *The presentation of self in everyday life*. Garden City, NY: Doubleday.

Goffman, E. (1967). *Interaction ritual: Essays on face-to-face behavior*. New York, NY: Doubleday.

Gonzales, N. M., & Campbell, M. (1994). Cocaine babies: Does prenatal exposure to cocaine affect development? *Journal of the American Academy of Child & Adolescent Psychiatry, 33*(1),16–19.

Gordon, L. (1988). *Heroes of their own lives: The politics and history of family violence*. New York, NY: Viking Press.

Gottesman, M. M. (2007). Infant crying: A clinical conundrum. *Journal of Pediatric Healthcare, 21*(5), 333–338.

Green, J. A. Gustafson, G. E., Irwin, J. R., & Kalinowski, L. L. (1995). Infant crying: Acoustics, perception, and communication. *Early Development and Parenting, 4*(4), 161–175.

Grey, D. J. R. (2015). 'Agonised weeping': Representing femininity, emotion, and infanticide in Edwardian newspapers. *Media History, 21*(4), 468–480.

Gurevich, L. (2008). Patriarchy? Paternalism? Motherhood discourses in trials of crimes against children. *Sociological Perspectives, 51*(3), 515–539.

Guttmacher Institute. (2016). *Unintended pregnancy in the United States*. Retrieved from https://www.guttmacher.org/fact-sheet/unintended-pregnancy-united-states.

Hays, S. (1996). *The cultural contradictions of motherhood*. New Haven, CT: Yale University Press.

Hegewisch, M. P., & Williams-Baron, E. (2017). *The gender wage gap by occupation and by race and ethnicity*. Institute for Women's Policy Research, IWPR#C456. https://iwpr.org/publications/gender-wage-gap-occupation-2016-race-ethnicity/.

Hewitson, M. (2000, July 29). Infanticide: Mothers who kill. *The New Zealand Herald*, p. C3.

Hochschild, A. R. (1989). *The second shift: Working parents and the revolution at home*. New York, NY: Viking.

Hochschild, A. R. (1997). *The time bind: When work becomes home and home becomes work*. New York, NY: Metropolitan Books.

Hunnicutt, G., & LaFree, G. (2008). Reassessing the structural covariates of cross-national infant homicide victimization. *Homicide Studies, 12*(1), 46–66.

Jackson, M. (2002). *Infanticide: Historical perspectives on child murder and concealment, 1550–2000*. Surrey: Ashgate.

Jambunathan, S., Burts, D. C., & Pierce, S. (2000). Comparisons of parenting attitudes among five ethnic groups in the United States. *Journal of Comparative Family Studies, 31*(4), 394–406.

Jensen, V. (2001). *Why women kill: Homicide and gender equality*. London: Lynne Reiner.

Kalil, A., & Ziol-Guest, K. (2013). *The Great Recession and married parents' use of time*. Stanford Center on Poverty & Inequality. Retrieved from https://inequality.stanford.edu/sites/default/files/media/_media/working_papers/kalil_zio-guest_great_recession_married_parents.pdf

Kaplan, H. B. (1986). *Social psychology of self-referent behavior*. New York, NY: Plenum.

Kline, M. (1995). Complicating the ideology of motherhood: Child welfare law and first nation women. In M. Fineman & I. Karpin (Eds.), *Mothers in law: Feminist theory and the legal regulation of motherhood.* (pp. 118–141). New York, NY: Columbia University Press.

Knight, B. (1991). *Forensic pathology.* New York, NY: Oxford University Press.

Korbin, J. E. (1986). Childhood histories of women imprisoned for fatal child maltreatment. *Child Abuse and Neglect, 10*(3), 331–338.

Kunz, J., & Bahr, S. J. (1996). A profile of parental homicide against children. *Journal of Family Violence, 11*(4), 347–362.

Lang, L. J. (2005). To love the babe that milks me: Infanticide and reconceiving the mother. *Columbia Journal of Gender & Law, 14*(2), 114–141.

Lareau, A. (2003). *Unequal childhoods: Class, race, and family life.* Berkeley, CA: U. C. Press.

LaRossa, R. (1986). *Becoming a parent.* Beverly Hills, CA: Sage.

Lemert, E. M. (1951). *Social pathology: A systematic approach to the theory of sociopathic behavior.* New York, NY: MacGraw-Hill.

Lerner, H. G. (1980). Internal prohibitions against female anger. *The American Journal of Psychoanalysis, 40*(2), 137–147.

Levitzky, S., & Cooper, R. (2001). *Infant Colic Syndrome: Maternal Fantasies of Aggression and Infanticide, 25*(2), 114–123.

Lewis, C. F., & Bunce, S. C. (2003). Filicidal mothers and the impact of psychosis on maternal filicide. *Journal of the American Academy of Psychiatry and Law, 31*(4), 459–470.

Lindsey, L. (2005). *Gender roles: A sociological perspective* (6th ed.). New York, NY: Routledge.

Loftin, C., & Parker, R. N. (1985). An errors-in-variable model of the effect of poverty on urban homicide rates. *Criminology, 23*(2), 269–287.

Luckenbill, D. (1977). Criminal homicide as a situated transaction. *Social Problems, 25*(1), 176–186.

Markus, H. (1977). Self-schemata and processing information about the self. *Journal of Personality and Social Psychology, 35*(2), 63–78.

Marx, K., & Engels, F. (1888 [1959]). *Marx and Engels: Basic writing on politics and philosophy.* In L. Feuer (Ed.). New York, NY: Doubleday Anchor.

Mattingly, M. J., & Bianchi, S. M. (2003). Gender differences in the quantity and quality of free time: The U. S. experience. *Social Forces, 81*(3), 999–1029.

Maushart, S. (1999). *The mask of motherhood: How becoming a mother changes everything and why we pretend it doesn't.* New York, NY: The New Press.

Mayfield, D. (1976). Alcoholism, alcohol, intoxication and assaultive behavior. *Diseases of the Nervous System, 37*(5), 288–291.

McCall, G. J., & Simmons, J. L. (1966). *Identities and interactions.* New York, NY: Free Press.

McGreier, D. J., & Azar, S. T. (2016). *Cognitive and transactional factors and punitive discipline: Associations with highly disadvantaged mother-child dyads.* Unpublished paper.

McLoyd, V. C. (1990). The impact of economic hardship on black families and children: Psychological distress, parenting, and socioemotional development. *Child Development, 61*(2), 331–346.

Mead, G. H. (1934). In C. W. Morris (Ed.), *Mind, self, and society*. Chicago, IL: University of Chicago Press.

Merton, R. (1938). Social structure and 'anomie'. *American Sociological Review*, *3*(5), 672–682.

Milkie, M., Mattingly, M. Nomagrechi, K. Bianchi, S. M., & Robinson, J. P. (2004). The time squeeze: Parental statuses and feelings about time with children. *Journal of Marriage and the Family*, *66*(3), 739–761.

Morrissey, B. (2003). *When women kill: Questions of agency and subjectivity*. London: Routledge.

Motz, A. (2001). *The psychology of female violence: Crime against the body*. Hove: Brunner-Routledge.

Mouzos, J. (2000). Homicidal encounters: A study of homicide in Australia, 1989–1999. *Australian Institute of Criminology Research and Public Policy Series, No. 28*. Canberra: Australia Institute of Criminology.

Mugavin, M. E. (2005). A meta-analysis of filicide classification systems: Psychosocial and psychodynamic issues in women who kill their children. *Journal of Forensic Nursing*, *1*(2), 65–72.

National Coalition Against Domestic Violence. (2015). *Domestic violence national statistics*. Retrieved from www.ncadv.org

National Crime Victims Survey. (2016, 2018). *Bureau of Justice Statistics*. Retrieved from https://www.bjs.gov/index.cfm?ty=dcdetail&iid=245

National Women's Law Center. (2018). *Equal pay and the wage gap*. Retrieved from https://nwlc.org/issue/equal-pay-and-the-wage-gap/

Nations, V. (2005). *Six-year follow-up evaluation of a home visitation program: The prevention of child abuse/neglect in an Alaska Native population*. Dissertation, University of Alaska, School of Social Work, Fairbanks, Alaska.

Newman, G. (1978). *The punishment response*. Philadelphia, PA: Lippincott.

Nuttbrock, L., & Freudiger, P. (1991). Identity salience and motherhood: A test of Stryker's theory. *Social Psychology*, *54*(2), 146–157.

Oakley, A. (1974). *Woman's work: The housewife, past and present*. New York, NY: Pantheon.

Oakley, A. (1974). *The sociology of housework*. New York, NY: Pantheon.

Oberman, M. (2003). Understanding infanticide in context: Mothers who kill, 1807–1930 and today. *The Journal of Criminal Law & Criminology*, *92*(3), 707–737.

Oberman, M., & Meyer, C. L. (2001). *Why mothers kill: Understanding the acts of moms from Susan Smith to the 'prom mom'*. New York, NY: NYU Press.

Oberman, M., & Meyer, C. L. (2008). *Why mothers kill: Interviews from prison*. New York, NY: NYU Press.

Ogle, R., Maier-Katkin, D., & Bernard, T. (1996). A theory of homicidal behavior among women. *Journal of Research on Crime and Delinquency*, *33*(2), 173–193.

Overpeck, M. D. (2003). Epidemiology of infanticide. In M. G. Spinelli (Ed.), *Infanticide: Psychosocial and legal perspectives on mothers who kill* (pp. 19–34). Washington, DC: American Psychiatric Publishing.

Parker, R. N. (1989). Poverty, subculture of violence, and type of homicide. *Social Forces*, *67*(4), 983–1007.

Pew Research Center. (2016). *Racial, gender wage gaps persist in U.S. despite some progress*. Retrieved from http://www.pewresearch.org/fact-tank/2016/07/01/racial-gender-wage-gaps-persist-in-u-s-despite-some-progress/

Radbill, S. (1987). Children in a world of violence: A history of child abuse. In R. Helfer & R. Kempe (Eds.), *The battered child* (4th ed., pp. 36–49). Chicago, IL: University of Chicago Press.

Renzetti, C. M., Curran, D. J., & Maier, S. L. (2012). *Women, men, and society* (6th ed.). New York, NY: Pearson.

Resnick, P. (1969). Child murder by parents: A psychiatric review of filicide. *American Journal of Psychiatry, 126*(3), 73–82.

Ridgeway, C. L. (2011). *Framed by gender: How inequality persists in the modern world.* New York, NY: Oxford University Press.

Rimm, D., Briddell, D., Zimmerman, M., & Caddy, G. (1981). The effects of alcohol and the expectancy of alcohol on snake fear. *Addictive Behaviors, 6*(1), 47–51.

Rodriguez, S. F., & Smithey, M. (1999). Infant and adult homicide: Incompatibility of predictive models. *Homicide Studies, 3*(2), 170–184.

Rose, L. (1986). *The massacre of the innocents: Infanticide in Britain 1800–1939.* London: Routledge and Kegan Paul.

Rossiter, A. (1988). *From private to public: A feminist exploration of early mothering.* Toronto: The Women's Press.

Rothman, B. K. (2000). *Recreating motherhood.* New York, NY: Routledge.

Sayer, L. C., Bianchi, S. M., & Robins, J. P. (2004). Are parents investing less in children? Trends in mothers' and fathers' time with children. *American Journal of Sociology, 110*(1), 1–43.

Schwartz, L. L., & Isser, N. K. (2007). *Child homicide: Parents who kill.* New York, NY: Taylor & Francis.

Scott, P. D. (1973). Fatal battered baby cases. *Medicine, Science, and the Law, 13*(3), 197–206.

Shaw, C. R., & McKay, H. D. (1969). *Juvenile delinquency and urban areas.* Chicago, IL: University of Chicago Press.

Sherman, R. (2017). Conflicted cultivation: Parenting privilege, and moral worth in wealthy New York families. *American Journal of Cultural Sociology, 5*(1–2), 1–33.

Shorter, E. (1975). *The making of the modern family.* New York, NY: Basic Books.

Stroud, J. (2008). A psychosocial analysis of child homicide. *Critical Social Policy, 28*(4), 482–505.

Smith-Loving, L., & McPherson, M. (1993). Birds of a feathery: Homophily in social networks. *Annual Review of Sociology, 27*(4), 415–444.

Smithey, M. (1994). *Infanticide: Toward a sociological perspective.* Dissertation, Texas A&M University, Department of Sociology, College Station, TX.

Smithey, M. (1997). Infant homicide at the hands of mothers: Toward a sociological perspective. *Deviant Behavior, 18*(3), 255–272.

Smithey, M. (1998). Infant homicide: Victim-offender relationship and causes of death. *Journal of Family Violence, 13*(3), 285–297.

Smithey, M. (2001). Maternal infanticide and modern motherhood. *Women & Criminal Justice, 13*(1), 65–83.

Smithey, M. (2018). *Survey on normative expectations of parenting, 2003-present.* Department of Sociology, Texas Tech University. Retrieved from http://www.myweb.ttu.edu/m.smithey

Smithey, M., & Ramirez, I. L. (2004). Suspicion of sudden infant death syndrome and injuries to infants: The effect of type of death certifier, training, and economics. *Deviant Behavior, 25*(5), 465–482.

Smithey, M., & Straus, M. (2003). Primary prevention of intimate partner violence. In H. Kury & J. Obergfell-Fuchs (Eds.), *Crime prevention: New approaches* (pp. 239–276). Mainz: Weisser-Ring.

Sobell, L. C., & Sobell, M. B. (1975). Drunkenness, a 'special circumstance' in crime and violence, sometimes. *International Journal of the Addictions, 10*(5), 869–882.

Sommers, I., & Baskin, D. (1993). The situation context of violent female offending. *Journal of Research on Crime & Delinquency, 30*(2), 136–162.

Stanton, J., & Simpson, A. (2002). Filicide: A review. *International Journal of Law and Psychiatry, 25*(1), 1–14.

Stanton, J., Simpson, A., & Wouldes, T. (2000). A qualitative study of filicide by mentally ill mothers. *Child Abuse & Neglect, 24*(11), 1451–1460.

Stanton, J., & Skipworth, J. (2005). Barriers to care in severe mental illness: Accounts from perpetrators intra-familial homicide. *Criminal Behaviour and Mental Health, 15*(3), 154–163.

Steele, B. F. (1987). Psychodynamic factors in child abuse. In K. Oates & A. C. Donnelly (Eds.), *Classic papers in child abuse*. Thousand Oaks, CA: Sage Publications.

Straus, M. A. (2001). *Beating the devil out of them: Corporal punishment in American families and its effects on children*. New Brunswick, NJ: Transaction Press.

Straus, M. A., & Gelles, R. J., (1990). *Physical violence in American families*. New York, NY: Routledge.

Stroud, J. (2008). European child homicide studies: Quantitative studies and a preliminary report on a complementary qualitative research approach. *Social Work in Europe, 7*(3), 31–37.

Stryker, S. (1968). Identity salience and role performance: The relevance of symbolic interaction theory for family research. *Journal of Marriage and the Family, 30*(4), 558–564.

Sutherland, E. H., & Cressey, D. R. (1960). *Principles of criminology* (6th ed.). Chicago, IL: J. B. Lippincott, Co.

Sutherland, J. (2010). Mothering, guilt, and shame. *Sociology Compass, 4*(5), 310–312.

Taylor, T. (2011). Re-examining cultural contradictions: Mothering ideology and the intersections of class, gender, and race. *Sociology Compass, 5*(10), 898–907.

Tittle, C. R. (1995). *Control balance: Toward a general theory of deviance*. New York, NY: Westview.

Totman, J. (1978). *The murderess: A psychosocial study of criminal homicide*. San Francisco, CA: R and E Research Associates.

Turner, R. (1978). The role and the person. *American Journal of Sociology, 84*(1), 1–23.

U. S. Census Bureau. (1990). *Texas*. Retrieved from https://www.census.gov/about/adrm/fsrdc/locations/texas.html

US Census Bureau. (2015). *American community survey*. Washington, DC. Retrieved from: https://www.census.goviprograms-surveysiacsi_guidanceicomparing-acs-data/2015.html

U. S. Department of Labor. (2015). *Time use survey*. Retrieved from https://www.bls.gov/tus/

U. S. Department of Labor. (2016). *An analysis of reasons for the disparity in wages between men and women*. CONSAD Research Corporation. Retrieved from

https://www.shrm.org/hr-today/public-policy/hr-public-policy-issues/Documents/Gender%20Wage%20Gap%20Final%20Report.pdf

von Hentig, H. (1948). *The criminal and his victim*. New Haven, CT: Yale University Press.

Wade, K., Black, A., & Ward-Smith, P. (2005). How mothers respond to their crying infant. *Journal of Public Health, 19*(6), 347–353.

Wall, G. (2001). Moral constructions of motherhood in breastfeeding discourse. *Gender and Society, 15*(4), 592–610.

Walmsley, J. (2000). Women and the Mental Deficiency Act of 1913: Citizenship, sexuality, and regulation. *British Journal of Learning Disabilities, 28*(2), 65–70.

Wandersman, L., Wandersman, A., & Kahn, S. (1980). Social support in the transition to parenthood. *Journal of Community Psychology, 8*(4), 332–342.

Warner, J. (2005). *Perfect madness: Motherhood in the age of anxiety*. New York, NY: Riverhead Books.

Widom, C. S. (1989). The cycle of violence. *Science, 244*(4901), 4899–4903.

Wolfgang, M. (1958). *Patterns of criminal homicide*. Philadelphia, PA: University of Pennsylvania Press.

Wynn, A. T. (2017). Gender, parenthood, and perceived chances of promotion. *Sociological Perspectives, 60*(4), 645–664.

Zeichner, A., & Pihl, R. O. (1979). Effects of alcohol and behavior contingencies on human aggression. *Journal of Abnormal Psychology, 88*(2), 153–160.

Zhu, W. X. (2003). The one child family policy. *Archives of Diseases in Children, 88*(6), 463–464.

Index

Printed in the United States
By Bookmasters